Encounters with Unjust Authority

The Dorsey Series in Sociology

Advisory Editor
Robin M. Williams, Jr.
Cornell University

Consulting Editor
Charles M. Bonjean
The University of Texas at Austin

Encounters with Unjust Authority

WILLIAM A. GAMSON
The University of Michigan

BRUCE FIREMAN
The University of California at Berkeley

STEVEN RYTINA
State University of New York

 1982

THE DORSEY PRESS   Homewood, Illinois   60430

ISBN 0-256-02746-3
Library of Congress Catalog Card No. 81–52438

Printed in the United States of America

1 2 3 4 5 6 7 8 9 0 ML 9 8 7 6 5 4 3 2

To those with the courage to say "No!"

Preface

In writing this book, we frequently told friends and acquaintances that we were studying encounters with unjust authority. The topic invariably brought a smile in response. It seems they were reminded of one or more incidents in their own lives. We have heard our share of hair-raising stories.

Not all of the stories fit our concern here. Many people described situations in which, as individuals, they were victimized by agents of some authority system. The situations that concerned us here were those in which a group of people confronted authority. We were interested in collective action.

In these group encounters, it was not always too clear whether one was a victim or a bystander. Frequently, it was a matter of choice. One can decide that it is someone else's problem and go along, or intervene in an attempt to prevent some injustice from occurring. Whether we think of the abuse as happening to *them* or to *us* is a matter of consciousness and identification. These things sometimes change in the course of encounters, and we will be exploring the process by which this happens.

Our explorations will involve a close analysis of three critical incidents in the growth of social movements. One of these involves a group of automobile workers who conducted a sit-down strike in General Motor's Fisher 1 plant in the winter of 1936–37. Another involves a group of students and community people who surrounded a police car in Berkeley, California, in the fall of 1964. The third involves an encounter between Malcolm X and his Temple Seven brethren of the Nation of Islam, and the Harlem police, in the early 1960s.

But the centerpiece of our analyses will be 33 fabricated encounters in which we created an unjust authority called the Manufacturers' Human Relations Consultants (MHRC). This organization hired people and tried to get them to help it use unfair tactics to win a legal case. These 33 encounters will be analyzed in minute detail to learn how some groups manage a successful rebellion career while others falter.

ACKNOWLEDGMENTS

We offer here an intellectual porridge of Tilly and Goffman. Charles Tilly is a suitable symbol for the roots of this study of groups that mobilized for collective action. Erving Goffman's work provided the inspiration for much of our analysis of ongoing interaction.

We have the usual indebtedness to supporting organizations that gave us the wherewithal to carry out the research described here. The National Science Foundation provided us with generous support under grant No. SOC 76–03045, "Group Formation for Collective Action."

The three of us worked with David Morgan and Bruce Taylor during two years of preparatory work and drafting of a research proposal to the NSF. We are greatly indebted to the supportive and intellectually exciting environment of the Center for Research on Social Organization at the University of Michigan, where we carried out this research. Graduate students and faculty colleagues, too numerous to mention, gave us helpful advice over the course of several years. The Center for Advanced Study in the Behavioral Sciences at Stanford and the Guggenheim Foundation provided Gamson with the time and the ideal environment to finish work that began in 1973. This is another of those books that might never have been written without the special ambience and time for reflection that the center provides.

The research itself was a collaborative one from the outset. We have already noted the joint nature of the research proposal that we developed with Morgan and Taylor, both of whom continued to contribute in numerous ways as the research progressed. Richard Cohn joined the research group a bit later and helped us to sharpen our design and polish our procedures during two critical years. Marge Bennett performed the heroic job of supervising the coding and maintaining necessary quality control in an extremely complex and difficult operation. Stanley Pressor and Jon Sell participated in the project for shorter periods; Pressor was especially helpful in the development of our questionnaires, and Sell's improvements in our technology reduced the amount of information that we had previously lost in recording the interaction. Mary Franklin and Ann Adams joined the project at a late stage but helped us in the development of codes for the videotaped interaction.

Throughout this project, but particularly in the coding stage, we were aided by a large number of undergraduates on work-study who watched video tapes for endless hours as they executed the codes that we developed. Finally, we owe an inestimable debt to the 260 men and women who served as potential challengers in our encounters with unjust authority and who taught us, through their words and deeds, how to mobilize for rebellious collective action.

William A. Gamson
Bruce Fireman
Steven Rytina

Contents

Micromobilization | 1

Management speedups were a widespread source of grievance among automobile and other industrial workers in America in the mid-1930s. A typical practice was the removal of one employee on a work team while maintaining the same production quota. Automobile workers were largely unorganized, but by 1936, brief sit-down strikes were becoming an increasingly common response. The handful of workers most directly affected by a speedup would stop working for a few minutes or hours until their grievance was settled in some fashion.

A typical incident of this sort occurred in the middle of November 1936 in a major General Motors plant in Flint, Michigan. It involved a team of welders on the swing shift at Fisher Body plant number 1. When they came on their shift, they discovered that one worker had been removed from the team. Two brothers named Perkins and another man, Joe Urban, simply stopped working.[1]

The foreman and superintendent came over to get them back to work, and a lengthy discussion followed over the speedup. While they were arguing, a sizable job gap developed on the assembly line before the men were finally persuaded to go back to work. When the Perkins brothers arrived for work the following evening they found their cards missing from the rack and notices: "Report to the employment office." In the office, they were paid off for their hours and given a red card, firing them.

---

[1] The account here is drawn from Kraus (1947) and Fine (1969). Kraus edited the *Flint Auto Worker* for the fledgling United Automobile Workers during the events described.

Neither the Perkins brothers nor Joe Urban were members of the struggling United Automobile Workers (UAW). In fact, the union could count on only 40 members among the 8,000 workers employed at Fisher 1. But there were a handful of union activists around on this occasion, and the Perkins brothers showed their red cards to some of them during the short lull before the shift began. The Perkins brothers headed home, but one of the union men, Bud Simons, took the initiative by running through the main welding and soldering department yelling, "The Perkins boys were fired! Nobody starts working!"

Kraus (1947: 48–54) describes the ensuing events in colorful detail:

> The whistle blew. Every man in the department stood at his station, a deep, significant tenseness in him. The foreman pushed the button, and the skeleton bodies, already partly assembled when they got to this point, began to rumble forward. But no one lifted a hand. All eyes were turned to Simons who stood out in the aisle by himself.
>
> The bosses ran about like mad.
>
> "Whatsamatter? Whatsamatter? Get to work!" they shouted.
>
> But the men acted as though they never heard them. One or two of them couldn't stand the tension. Habit was deep in them, and it was like physical agony for them to see the bodies pass untouched. They grabbed their tools and chased after them. "Rat! Rat!" the men growled without moving, and the others came to their senses.
>
> The superintendent stopped by the "bow-men."
>
> "You're to blame for this!" he snarled.
>
> "So what if we are?" little Joe Urban, the Italian, cried, overflowing with pride. "You ain't running your line, are you?"
>
> That was altogether too much. The superintendent grabbed Joe and started for the office with him. The two went down the entire line, while the men stood rigid as though awaiting the word of command. . . . Simons, a torch-solderer, was almost at the end of the line. He too was momentarily held in vise by the superintendent's overt act of authority. The latter had dragged Joe Urban past him when he finally found the presence of mind to call out:
>
> "Hey, Teefee, where you going?"
>
> It was spoken in just an ordinary conversational tone, and the other was taken so aback he answered the really impertinent question.
>
> "I'm taking him to the office to have a little talk with him." Then suddenly he realized and got mad. "Say, I think I'll take you along too!"
>
> That was his mistake.
>
> "No you won't!" Simons said calmly.
>
> "Oh yes I will!" and he took hold of his shirt.
>
> Simons yanked himself loose.
>
> And suddenly, at this simple act of insurgence, Teefee realized his danger. He seemed to become acutely conscious of the long line of silent men and felt the threat of their potential strength. They had been transformed into something he had never known before and over which he

no longer had any command. He let loose of Simons and started off again with Joe Urban, hastening his pace. Simons yelled:

"Come on, fellows, don't let him fire little Joe!"

About a dozen boys shot out of line and started after Teefee. The superintendent dropped Joe like a hot poker and deer-footed it for the door. The men returned to their places and all stood waiting. . . . The moment tingled with expectancy.

Teefee returned shortly, accompanied by Bill Lynch, the assistant plant manager who approached Simons. Simons suggested that the workers get a committee together to see the plant manager, Evan Parker, and Lynch agreed. Simons was not able to exercise complete control over who was included on the committee but put together a largely pro-union group. As Kraus (1947) describes it:

. . . Evan Parker, the plant manager, greeted them as smooth as silk. "You can smoke if you want to, boys," he said as he bid them to take the available chairs. "Well, what seems to be the trouble here? We ought to be able to settle this thing."

"Mr. Parker, it's the speedup the boys are complaining about," Simons said, taking the lead. "It's absolutely beyond human endurance. And now we've organized ourselves into a union. It's the union you're talking to right now, Mr. Parker."

"Why that's perfectly all right, boys," Parker said affably. "Whatever a man does outside the plant is his own business."

The men were almost bowled over by this manner. They had never known Parker as anything but a tough, cold tomato with an army sergeant's style. He was clearly trying to play the weaker boys on the committee and began asking them leading questions. Simons or Walt Moore [Simons' close friend and political ally] would try to break in and answer for them.

"Now I didn't ask you," Parker would say, "you can talk when it's your turn." In this way, he sought to split the committee up into so many individuals. Simons realized he had to put an end to that quickly.

"We might as well quit talking right now, Mr. Parker," he said, putting on a tough act. "Those men have got to go back and that's all there is to it!"

"That's what you say," Parker snapped back.

"No, that's what the men say. You can go out and see for yourself. Nobody is going to work until that happens."

. . . The plant manager seemed to soften again. All right, he said, he'd agree to take the two men back if he found their attitude was okay.

"Who's to judge that?" Simons asked.

"I will, of course!"

"Uh-uh!" Simons smiled and shook his head.

The thing bogged down again. Finally, Parker said the Perkins brothers could return unconditionally on Monday. [It was Friday night]. . . . To make this arrangement final, he agreed that the workers in the department would get paid for the time lost in the stoppage. But Simons held fast to the original demand. . . .

"They go back tonight," he insisted.

Parker was fit to be tied. What was this? Never before in his life had he seen anything like it.

"Those boys have left!" he shouted. "It might take hours to get them back. Are you going to keep the lines tied up all that time?"

"We'll see what the men say," Simons replied.

The committee went back to the shop and held an impromptu meeting, which ended with strong support to sit down until the Perkins brothers were back at work. When Parker got the news of the strike vote, he contacted the police to bring the Perkins boys in. One of them was out and took a few hours to locate before they returned to "a deafening cheer that could be heard in the most distant reaches of the quarter-mile-long plant." (Kraus, 1947: 54).

This incident had immediate consequences. "The news of what had transpired in Fisher Body 1 on November 13, this minor but clear-cut victory over a powerful employer, had an electrifying effect on Flint's auto-workers," Fine writes. "By the end of the month, the Flint UAW, whose paid-up membership was probably not in excess of 150 at the end of October, had a membership of 1,500, most of it concentrated in the two Fisher Body plants" (1969: 117). By the end of the year, two months later, the great GM sit-down strike of 1936–37 was underway. This strike, which Fine (1969) calls "the most significant American labor conflict in the twentieth century," had its strongest sustained support among the workers of Fisher 1.

Growth following such an incident does not take place in some mystical fashion. Clearly, it was a lively topic of conversation during those ensuing two weeks. Lessons were drawn in these conversations as the events were framed and interpreted through networks of face-to-face interaction. "The Fisher 1 boys began bringing friends into the union from Fisher 2, Buick and Chevrolet," writes Kraus (1947).

The incident described took place in a supportive historical context. Ten days before it occurred, Roosevelt's overwhelming electoral victory over Alfred M. Landon had boosted the morale of workers. Michigan had elected a governor, Frank Murphy, who was considered sympathetic to labor. "The election" said a CIO leader in Detriot, "is a mandate to labor to organize." Sit-down strikes were occurring with increasing frequency. Fine (1969) reports 48 strikes in 1936 of at least one day, with 22 of these lasting more than 24 hours. Major CIO organizing drives were underway in several industries. Workers in Flint knew about this activity, and it provided a framework for interpreting the specific incidents described.

Operating within this supportive context, individual union activists were able to carry out their strength-in-unity theme into a variety of interactions. The small group of union men in Fisher 1 were ready for some incident of this sort. Three days before the November 13 strike, a local UAW organizer, Robert Travis, had met with the 40 UAW members in the plant. Travis instructed them on "how to act in case of surprise developments, how they were to come together at a given spot in each plant, reach a quick decision, and take appropriate steps. He gave each of the men a 'volunteer organizer' card with the international seal and the signature of the officers on it." (Kraus, 1947: 45). The incident described provided an opportunity for such men to spread their political consciousness among workers more generally.

As worker consciousness was being shaped, so were worker loyalties to a particular collective actor—the UAW. It was Simons, a union activist, who yelled, "Nobody starts working!" and Simons who put his own job on the line in confronting the superintendent. The risks taken by Simons and other union activists on behalf of other workers asserted the claim of the union as the appropriate vehicle for collective action. Their actions helped to convince potential members that the union should be taken seriously as an instrument of collective action, that it was becoming an effective organization. The encounter produced a twin message—that there was strength in unity and that the UAW was the appropriate instrument for collective action.

MOBILIZATION FOR COLLECTIVE ACTION

When the Fisher 1 episode occurred, neither the automobile companies nor any other major power holder in American society recognized the UAW and dealt with it as an agent of automobile workers. The union faced the task of organizing an aggregate of individual, unorganized workers from many different backgrounds spread among plants in several cities.

For several years, the UAW engaged in a bitter struggle to win acceptance as the agent for the collective interests of automobile workers and to gain benefits for this constituency. In the course of the struggle, the capacity of automobile workers for collective action greatly increased. In a word, they *mobilized.*

This process of mobilization took place over several years, involving many encounters in many places. Some of these were *critical incidents,* by which we mean any encounter leading to a sudden, discontinuous change in the capacity for collective action—either an increase or decrease. The Fisher 1 episode serves well to illustrate such encounters because of the availability of an unusually detailed narrative account.

A critical incident should serve as a red flag for students of mobilization for collective action, since long-term processes that affect mobilization are being altered in some fashion. A close examination of critical incidents ought to increase our understanding of just what it is that increases or decreases the capacity for collective action.

But there is a second, more subtle reason why the Fisher 1 encounter warrants our attention. Although it took place in a matter of hours, it contained a microcosm of many long-term mobilization processes. Potential challengers were grappling, over the hours, with problems that are microversions of those that social movement organizations grapple with over the years.

1. Long-term challengers, in their effort to mobilize, frequently must contend with dominant belief systems or ideologies that sustain and legitimize established social and political institutions. Potential challengers must break the sway such belief systems hold in their constituency if they hope eventually to gain a commitment to a belief system that supports collective action for change.

2. Social movement organizations frequently find that they are competing with their antagonists, the authorities, for the loyalties of the people whom they are attempting to mobilize. Political socialization that encourages obedience to authority and supporting cultural belief systems may make the bonds of authority a major obstacle to unauthorized collective action. To succeed, challengers must loosen the bonds by delegitimizing the authority that is the target of their challenge.

3. Long-term mobilization efforts must be sustained by some organization. The social movement organizations carrying the challenge may be very loose, with no very clear boundary between members and supporters. Or they may, at the other extreme, require a long probationary period and an exacting initiation ritual before one becomes a member. Whatever the form, these organizations face a series of internal control problems that they must solve in order to succeed.

The most central of these organizational problems is what Selznick (1960) calls "transforming a voluntary association into a managerial structure. . . . Put most simply, the process referred to is one which changes *members* into *agents*, transforms those who merely give consent into those (at an extreme, soldiers) who do work as well as conform." No simple task. The challenging organization must build commitment when people's personal interests may have priority and when their loyalties may belong to rival organizations or factions.

Typically, the challenger must accomplish this transfer of loyalties in the context of hostility and attempted repression by authorities and other groups threatened by the changes being sought. One measure of successful mobilization is the challenger's ability to gain the willingness of members to promote and defend it qua organization—that is, a loyalty to the organization itself and not simply to the goals it is pursuing.

All of these long-term processes of mobilization have their counterparts in certain encounters. Indeed, some would argue that one *must* study such microevents to adequately specify the process of macromobilization. As Collins puts it, "Macrophenomena are made up of aggregations and repetitions of many similar micro-events . . . [therefore], sociological concepts can be made fully empirical only by grounding them in a sample of the typical micro-events that make them up" (1981: 988).

In some encounters, one can observe the participants in a process of reinterpreting events. They abandon one definition of the situation and adopt a new one that supports some form of unauthorized collective action. In some encounters, one can observe the participants breaking out of their sense of obligation to comply with authorities who they are not at all sure deserve compliance. In some encounters, one can observe an aggregate of people developing a sense of group solidarity; individual members become increasingly ready to take personal risks on behalf of the group as a whole.

Not all of these processes are likely to be present in any single encounter, but in some special cases one has a good opportunity to observe all of them operating to some degree. The Fisher 1 incident is an example of such a case—a virtual microcosm of a group mobilizing for collective action. In studying it and others like it, one can observe mobilization in miniature.

MACROMOBILIZATION AND MICROMOBILIZATION

This book is rooted in a relatively new approach to the study of social movements: resource mobilization.[2] Until the early 1970s, the study of social movements was dominated by "breakdown" theories. Social movements, in the old view, are one product of social disorganization; other products include suicide, criminal behavior, and additional symptoms of a social system in trouble. The anger and other emotional expressions of participants are signals of the stresses and strains of society. People are reacting, frequently violently, without really understanding the larger social forces that buffet them.

The breakdown theorists differ in their emphases on just what is responsible for social disorganization, but the rapid rate of social

---

[2] Good general statements of this approach are found in Tilly (1978), McCarthy and Zald (1977), and Oberschall (1973). Paradigmatic empirical studies include Shorter and Tilly (1974), Gamson (1975), Snyder and Kelly (1976), and Aminzade (1977). Jenkins (1981) contains a good critical review of more traditional approaches from a resource mobilization perspective. Zald and McCarthy (1979) provide a representative collection of work by different authors flowing from this approach, including a number of critical examinations of resource mobilization theory by persons sympathetic to the general approach.

change is generally at the core. As Jenkins (1981) summarizes it, "Rapid economic development destroys the traditional sources of social cohesion and integration, thereby causing a 'breakdown' in the sociopolitical order that in turn gives rise to the discontents underlying movements and a wide variety of other 'disorderly' actions. Participants in social movements are the uprooted."

Resource mobilization theory provides a counterpoint. The uniting theme in work stemming from this approach is the rejection of breakdown theories. Social change remains of central importance from the resource mobilization viewpoint, but for different reasons than in breakdown theories. Changes in the social and economic structure of society affect the interests and relative power of contending parties in the political arena. Changes create new opportunities for collective action and repression, or new threats to the interests of potential challengers and authorities.

Breakdown theories do not give much credit to social movements as attempts to achieve collective goals by mobilizing resources and employing strategies of influence. In the resource mobilization approach, the American Medical Association and Students for a Democratic Society (SDS) are not different species, but members of the same species faced with different political environments. Social movement organizations are engaged in interactions characterized by a high degree of conflict. To understand events, one must analyze both the collective action of the challengers and the social control efforts of their authority targets—both have interests and employ strategies in pursuit of them. The course that social movements follow is a product of this interaction.

The discontented are no more and no less rational than other political actors. Rebellion, in the resource mobilization perspective, is simply politics by other means. Even violence is not an eruption of latent tensions and frustrations that takes place in an organizational vacuum, but an outcome of a continuous process of mobilization and conflictful interaction. Tilly (1973) observes that collective violence is one of the commonest forms of political participation and suggests several reasons why one should hesitate "to assume that collective violence is a sort of witless release of tension divorced from workaday politics: its frequent success as a tactic, its effectiveness in establishing or maintaining a group's political identity, its normative order, its frequent recruitment of ordinary people, and its tendency to evolve in cadence with peaceful political action."

We share the underlying assumptions of the resource mobilization approach, but recognize its incompleteness. It has not been particularly strong on the role of ideas and political consciousness in shaping collective action. Nor has it paid much attention to how long-term mobilization processes are mediated and altered in face-to-face interaction. Resource mobilization has neglected social psychology.[3]

A bit of history makes it easy enough to see why. Not many years ago, the field of social movements was virtually unchallenged turf for social psychologists. Breakdown theories are, in large part, social psychology theories. Social psychologists were able to illuminate the frustration caused by relative deprivation and thereby to identify the mechanism by which social disorganization leads to social movements and other forms of collective behavior.

From a resource mobilization perspective, this heavy emphasis on the psychological state of movement participants is a misplaced one. "We want to move," McCarthy and Zald (1977) argue, "from a strong assumption about the centrality of deprivation and grievances to a weak one, which makes them a component, indeed, sometimes a secondary component in the generation of social movements. . . . Grievances and discontent may be defined, created, and manipulated by issue entrepreneurs and organizations." They advise us to worry less about the hearts and minds of the constituency and more about the structure and strategy of the organizations that carry the movement.

But resource mobilization theory needs its own, more appropriate social psychology, focusing less on sources of frustration and more on the cognitive and face-to-face interaction processes involved in mobilizing for collective action. Social psychology is an indispensable component of an adequate theory of resource mobilization, not an antagonist of it. It deserves recognition as a legitimate partner, concerned with illuminating a set of microprocesses that operate in the mobilization of resources for collective action. We use the term *micromobilization* as a label for this set of concerns.

THE STUDY OF ENCOUNTERS

A great deal of general social psychology can be applied in a relatively straightforward fashion to micromobilization. What social psy-

---

[3] Not completely. There has been a good deal of recognition of the role of face-to-face interaction in recruiting for social movement organizations. Gerlach and Hine (1970) present a persuasive case for the proposition that the key to the spread of a social movement can be "found in the process of face-to-face recruitment by committed participants." Ross (1978) addresses the role of primary groups not only in recruitment but also in passing on organizational traditions and ideology and, ultimately, in influencing internal decision making, strategies of collective action, and how the movement organization responds to external crises. Turner and Killian (1972) have much to say on the role of primary groups in building and maintaining commitment to social movement organizations. Schmeidler (1980), in discussing the role of ideas in collective action, is an excellent exception to the general lack of attention that subject receives in the resource mobilization perspective.

chologists have to say about how individuals develop commitments to collective entities, about the flow of influence and communication in interpersonal interaction, about group process and persuasive communication—all can be said about the operation of social movement organizations. A distinctive subfield of micromobilization must concentrate on what is special about these processes in mobilization for collective action.

The study of micromobilization, we suggest, should center on the encounter. We use the term *encounter* as Goffman (1961) does, to mean a focused gathering. Encounters differ from other kinds of face-to-face interaction in a number of important respects. They have a single focus of attention. There is a heightened awareness of the mutual relevance of each others' acts.

Encounters have a definite beginning and end, usually marked by some ceremony or ritual expression. The beginning frequently involves some act creating a common focus of attention—for example, the pounding of a gavel or a verbal call for attention. Sometimes an unanticipated event will create the common focus that marks the beginning of an encounter. Ends of encounters are delineated in like manner, with a signaled termination of the common focus. Think of an encounter, then, as a continuous bounded strip of focused activity.

The Fisher 1 episode consisted of a string of important encounters. One might begin with the meeting three days before the firing when local UAW organizer Travis met with 40 UAW members from the plant. The dramatic confrontation between Superintendent Teefee and Bud Simons was the next major scene. The negotiation session with the plant manager, Parker, provided another encounter of a different type. The impromptu meeting back in the shop in which a strike vote was held was yet another important encounter, with its own set of challenges.

Different processes are highlighted by different kinds of encounters. To exhaust the study of micromobilization, one would need to analyze all of the following types:

1. *Recruitment meetings.* These encounters focus on the mobilization of support from a constituency. The challengers are attempting to gain adherents plus the resources and energy that they can provide. The major parties are those who are already active and represent the movement organization and those who are potential supporters.

Issues of political consciousness and symbolism are highlighted in such encounters. The choice of symbols by a movement organization is of major significance. What are the consequences, for example, of choosing a symbol that emphasizes continuity with the past rather than a sharp break with it? What solidarities are invoked through the political language that is used? What rituals are employed, with what effects?

2. Internal meetings.   These encounters focus on which strategies of mobilization or influence should be pursued. The participants are cadre and potential cadre of the movement organization. There are no outside parties—or, at least, none known as such to most of the participants.

Issues of generating and maintaining commitment are highlighted in such encounters. Many movement organizations, for example, have ideological beliefs that support widespread member participation and consensual decision making. To be effective, they need to avoid interminable and enervating meetings that burn out their cadre, turn away supporters, and accomplish nothing. The willingness of participants to come to meetings and work for the organization in the future will be affected by how this dilemma is handled.

3. Encounters with the media.   This interaction has the following dynamic. Representatives of a movement organization are attempting to frame the movement and its carriers in a particular fashion—emphasizing certain features and deemphasizing or denying others. They intend, by presenting themselves through the media in a particular way, to create and maintain a supportive climate for their efforts to mobilize their constituency and influence their target.

The media representatives in turn, have their own agenda and operating norms. They have a limited set of scenarios for treating movement organizations and are frequently skeptical or even hostile to a group's attempt to present itself. It is precisely this intricate relationship that Gitlin (1977, 1980) and Molotch (1979) explore in illuminating the subtle ways in which the civil rights, antiwar, and other movements were altered through the interaction of movement and media.[4]

4. Encounters with allies.   These interactions focus on coalition formation—the pooling of resources in joint collective action. Potential allies must reach agreements on many delicate matters. What will the form and nature of the action be? What will each party contribute? How will credit be shared? Or perhaps even, should the separate partners merge into a single organization?

Issues of internal cohesion and loyalty are highlighted in such encounters. Coalition agreements and mergers inevitably involve some

---

[4] It is worth distinguishing these two-party encounters from the even more complicated case where media representatives are present to witness another kind of encounter. These dual-focus encounters require a deft balancing act on the part of movement spokesmen to satisfy competing objectives.

compromise and adjustment of priorities. While outsiders may see barely perceptible differences between members of a coalition, some insiders may see a fundamental divergence in doctrine or program that makes such a coalition unconscionable. Encounters with allies then, frequently test a group's ability to hold on to its existing support and avoid factional splits.

5. *Encounters with countermovement groups.* These encounters focus on the strategy and tactics of conflict. When challengers confront an antagonist who is actively working against them, their objective must be to neutralize or weaken this adversary.

Challengers must consider how their strategies of waging political conflict affect their own internal support. A ploy that effectively discredits the opposition is not an effective one if it succeeds in embarrassing and discrediting the challenger as well. Issues of mobilization complicate an apparent two-party conflict by forcing both sides to consider how their actions will be received by their own supporters.

Interesting as they are, we will not be exploring these types of encounters here. All of our attention will center on a sixth kind of encounter—one in which potential challengers confront people in authority.

Encounters with authorities | 2

Encounters with authorities, which are the core of micromobilization, are especially likely to furnish critical incidents for long-term mobilization. They provide the contending parties with opportunities for a variety of heroics and confound them with difficult dilemmas that have no ready solution. Reputations are won and lost in such encounters.

Because encounters are face-to-face gatherings with a single focus of attention, there is a heightened awareness of the mutual relevance of other participants' stances and actions. The initiation and justification of various tactics by challengers and their reaction to various countermeasures by authorities are highly visible. Proponents of alternative lines of action joust: the support for challengers and authorities waxes and wanes, and the results are immediately apparent to those present to help them decide their own course of action.

We distinguish two important subtypes among encounters with authority. In one type, a group of participants gather in the same place to press some claim against authorities. The gathering is at the initiative of the potential challengers, although it may have been unintentionally precipitated by the action of authorities. Perhaps a group of striking workers block the main gate of a plant to prevent substitute workers from entering, and police attempt to remove them. Or a group of citizens march to the Winter Palace to petition the tsar for redress and encounter troops that fire upon them. Or a collection of people, incensed by the arrest of a comrade, gather at a common meeting place where authorities attempt to disperse them. Tilly (1978) calls these encounters "contentious gatherings."[1]

---

[1] In fact, authorities need not be present for an encounter to qualify as a contentious gathering. A group of workers holding a rally to protest some company action would qualify, even if it were a purely internal encounter with neither management nor law enforcement officials present.

13

Our focus here is on a second, more innocent subtype. Imagine a situation that is defined from the outset as an *authority encounter*. The participants recognize that one party claims the right to regulate some aspect of the behavior of other participants—that is, there is some agent of authority present. Participants are gathered not to press some claim but for some other purpose, perhaps to carry out some task set by the authority system in which they are operating. At the beginning of such encounters, participants are in a state of compliance.

The confrontation in Fisher 1 is an example. The participants gathered, not to press a claim, but to assemble automobiles at the behest of General Motors. They all recognized the foreman and superintendent as agents of management who claimed the right to regulate the work of other participants. They entered the encounter ready to honor the claim—that is, they took it for granted.

In the end, many participants resisted the claim on this occasion, but that marks this as an unusual authority encounter. Indeed, our daily lives are filled with encounters with authority that run a smooth course and have no special interest for the study of micromobilization. They become interesting for our purposes only when an additional condition is met: the presence of an *injustice frame* as an interpretation of what is happening in the encounter.

By an *injustice frame,* we mean a belief that *the unimpeded operation of the authority system, on this occasion, would result in an injustice.* To qualify as an encounter with unjust authority, one or more of the participants must adopt this frame. The belief may be held privately and by only a small minority. It may originate in a belief that predates the encounter or arise in the course of it because agents of authority act in a questionable and unexpected manner. For our purposes, the presence of any who adopt this injustice frame introduces the risk of moving the whole set of participants to unauthorized collective action. They become potential challengers.

In speaking of unjust authority, then, we do not assert our own moral judgment as some sort of general standard for all to adopt. We take the standpoint of the participants—it is their perceptions of potential injustice that makes the encounter problematic. The degree to which participants eventually submit to regulation is at issue in such encounters. In ordinary encounters with authority, compliance is not an issue, since participants are quite comfortable acting as they are expected to and have no reason for not complying. Once present, the injustice frame may spread and become generally shared. Further, it may eventually become the supporting belief for some form of rebellion.[2]

---

[2] It is not disapproval of authority as such but a particular kind of disapproval that makes the encounter relevant. An injustice involves the violation of some shared princi-

Earlier, we singled out three long-term mobilization processes that can be studied at the level of the encounter: (*a*) the process of replacing a dominant belief system that legitimizes the status quo with an alternative, mobilizing belief system that supports collective action for change, (*b*) the process of removing the bonds of obligation that constituents of a social movement organization may feel toward the authority system against which some unauthorized collective action is directed, and (*c*) the process of building commitment to social movement organizations that are engaged in mobilization efforts. A closer look at the relevant micromobilization processes will demonstrate why encounters with unjust authority offer an especially rich microcosm.

1. Adopting an injustice frame. Encounters in general are governed by a primary framework that defines the nature of the occasion. In most encounters, this primary frame is noncontroversial and not an issue. All of the participants at weddings or classroom encounters, for example, normally take for granted such a primary frame. As Goffman points out (1974: 21), people are "likely to be unaware of such organized features as the framework has and unable to describe the framework with any completeness if asked, yet these handicaps are no bar to [their] easily and fully applying it." They act in terms of it, doing the things appropriate for weddings, and not classrooms, when they go to weddings.

Encounters with authority have an additional, special property: those acting in authority roles assume the right to define the penumbra of social expectations that surround the primary framework. Furthermore, it is the highest ranking authority present in the encounter who assumes this right unless it is explicitly delegated.

Normally, we don't care about such perquisites of authority and take them for granted. In encounters with unjust authority, however, these perquisites become extremely important. The primary frame is itself part of the issue between potential challengers and authorities. The normal perquisites of authority give hegemony to the frame that authorities present in such encounters. Would-be challengers face the problem of overcoming a definition of the situation that they themselves may take as part of the natural order.

Challengers can, of course, make the primary frame a matter of contention through their words or actions. They may force authorities to enter into de facto negotiations in spite of a primary frame that presents the challengers as obliged to accept some form of regulation. They may take unilateral actions that imply or proclaim an injustice

---

ple about what is fair—that is, it involves a violation of some moral code. It may not always be easy to know how participants view an authority system, since there are powerful reasons why people comply in spite of disapproving of what they are asked to do. Clearly, one cannot infer their view of authority simply by observing their behavior but must rely on other, independent evidence.

frame. When an injustice frame becomes the basis for collective action during an encounter, we have an opportunity to observe its spread and eventual adoption as it is happening.

2. *Breaking the bonds of authority.* "The first step any person must take to reconceive authority is to disengage from it temporarily," Sennett writes (1980: 134). A mental state in which one feels obliged to honor the claims of authority is an extremely difficult one from which to launch unauthorized collective action. A series of forces hold one in role, making compliance the natural state. Milgram (1974: 133) argues that there is a tendency for those in such a role to develop a particular mental set or state of consciousness that he calls the "agentic state." It is a condition a person is in

> . . . when he sees himself as an agent for carrying out another person's wishes. This term will be used in opposition to that of *autonomy*—that is, when a person sees himself as acting on his own. . . . A person entering an authority system no longer views himself as acting out of his own purposes but rather comes to see himself as an agent for executing the wishes of another person. Once an individual conceives his action in this light, profound alterations occur in his behavior and his internal functioning.

This state of consciousness, Milgram suggests, removes from the individual the sense of responsibility for his own actions. As an agent of another's will, one is no longer choosing but simply carrying out a set of well-defined expectations.

Just how compelling such a state is depends on the nature of one's role in the authority system. Engagement is likely to be highest for agents such as managers or enforcers, somewhat less for agents such as employees, and weaker still for those in such general public roles as spectator. Even when the bonds holding one in role in an authority encounter are at their weakest, however, participants must still go through a process of disengagement before rebellious action can occur.

Breaking the bonds of authority requires active effort. As Moore points out, "There are too many potent social and psychological mechanisms that can prevent human beings not only from expressing moral outrage at their situation but sometimes even from feeling it. There is no guarantee that exploitation, or just plain human misery, will somehow secrete its own antidote. Human beings have to create their own moral standards of condemnation and their own forms of collective action in order to change such situations" (1978: 457). One can witness, in the course of the encounter, the process by which potential challengers discredit agents of the authority system and undermine authority's claims of obligation from participants.

3. *Organizing a challenger.* The potential challengers in an en-

counter with unjust authority may be variously organized. In some cases, they may be passersby, attracted to the encounter fortuitously by some dramatic event. In other cases, they may be a disciplined group of comrades with marshalls to guide their collective action. Whatever their level of prior organization, they must face a series of organizational issues as they attempt to respond collectively in a fluid interaction situation. Even in well-planned contentious gatherings, the responses of authorities cannot be predicted in detail, and much improvisation may become necessary.

Challengers must have some mechanism, however informal, for selecting courses of action. In some cases, the mechanism is not informal at all but consists of a well-developed alternative authority system, with certain group members designated as having the right to give orders on what course of action to take. In other cases, the mechanism may be as informal as allowing certain exemplars to seize the initiative. Or it might involve a discussion from which a consensual line of action emerges. By whatever mechanism, the group must be able to make collective decisions.

Challengers must also maintain enough social control over their constituency to make the collective decisions stick. In some cases, the mechanism of social control may rest on a web of voluntarily accepted and shared obligations. In other cases, it may rest on the fear of negative sanctions or the lure of personal advantage. By whatever mechanism, challengers must be prevented from breaking ranks in a way that makes the line of action chosen impossible to carry out.

These organizational problems are particularly acute when the potential challengers begin as an aggregate of individuals with little sense of solidarity and organizational infrastructure. If, in the course of the encounter, they become a cohesive operating unit, we have an opportunity to observe the emergence of a nascent social movement organization as it is happening.

4. *Some caveats.*   Not all of these transformations will occur in any given encounter with unjust authority. One learns from the variance among them—from the failures and partial successes as well as from such triumphs as realized at Fisher 1. But many processes in macromobilization are absent in micromobilization. There is an analogy between a primary framework governing an encounter and political ideology more generally. But it does not extend to the role of the mass media, for example, in shaping political consciousness, for there is no counterpart of the media in an encounter. The challengers in an encounter need not worry about such problems as sustaining the commitment of their constituency during periods when members are not actively engaged in movement activity. The creation and management of coalitions with other organizations, the development of movement

cadre, the problems of leadership succession and many other organizational issues have no useful analogue in encounters with unjust authority. Our claim is a more modest one—that the parallels between the most central problems faced in encounters with unjust authority and those faced in a sustained challenge are rich enough to suggest that many of the solutions follow a similar process.

CONTRASTS AMONG ENCOUNTERS

Milgram (1974) designed a fabrication to explore a number of fundamental issues underlying obedience to authority. The paradigmatic situation that Milgram created involves a subject who is asked to administer what he believes to be an increasingly painful and, perhaps, dangerous series of electric shocks to an innocent victim. The person doing the asking plays the role of a psychologist conducting experimental work on how punishment affects learning.

Milgram was studying an individual encounter with unjust authority, but our concern is with micromobilization, a collective process. "Disobedience," Walzer argues, "when it is not criminally but morally, religiously, or politically motivated, is almost always a collective act, and it is justified by the values of the collectivity and the mutual engagements of its members" (1970: 4). Much can be learned from the individual encounter that Milgram created, but many additional processes emerge when a group of participants with a similar relationship to an authority system confront its agents. Solidarity of participants, problems of coordinating common action, the degree of consensus about what is happening and what should be done about it, all take on major importance. Collective rebellion reflects or presages the emergence of some collective entity that can sustain a rebellious state beyond the immediate encounter.

The big story in the Milgram fabrication is the very substantial amount of compliance by a broad range of people under a variety of conditions. Our scenario has a different theme. We compare groups that differ in their degree of successful mobilization, but we have very few tales of general compliance to tell. The differences between individual and collective encounters are so massive that it should come as no surprise that our tagline is quite different from Milgram's.

An analysis of these collective encounters must begin with a consideration of the important parameters affecting micromobilization. The major ones may be conveniently grouped under (a) the organization and assets of potential challengers, (b) the organization and assets of authorities, and (c) the legitimacy of authorities.

Organization and assets of potential challengers. Potential challengers may differ enormously in their prior organization and in the resources and know-how that they individually bring to the encounter. To illustrate, consider the contrast among the challengers in the following two encounters.

In the fall of 1964, students at the University of California's Berkeley campus gathered for a rally in front of the campus administration building, Sproul Hall. It was an early stage in the emerging Berkeley free speech movement. Eight students had been suspended on the previous day for deliberately violating a university ban against political activity on campus grounds. About an hour and a half before the rally was scheduled to begin, a campus civil rights activist named Jack Weinberg set up a political table in the forbidden area in front of Sproul Hall. He was shortly confronted by the administration in the person of Dean Murphy. Media reporters were on hand. Heirich (1971), who gives a detailed account of the encounter that day, managed to reconstruct much of the following conversation from a radio station KPFA tape:

Murphy: Are you prepared to remove yourself, *and* the table from university property?

Weinberg [*very quietly*]: I'm not prepared.

Murphy: Are you aware that by not doing so you are subjecting yourself to probable disciplinary action?

Weinberg [*still more quietly*]: I—uh—I'm aware that you're going to do what you'll try to do.

Murphy: All right. Will you—uh—identify yourself?

Weinberg: No.

Murphy [*in a dead-pan voice, almost as if he were reading a script instead of talking to a particular person*]: I must inform you if you are a student you are violating university regulations, and if you are a nonstudent you are violating the trespass law. Will you identify yourself?

Weinberg [*even more quietly*]: No, I will not.

Murphy: You leave me no alternative but to ask Lieutenant Chandler to arrest you. Lieutenant Chandler, would you please arrest him.

Chandler: You come with me, then, please.

Voices: Take their place!

Weinberg, following classic civil rights tactics, did not either assist nor resist the arrest, requiring that several officers carry him to a nearby police car. The police were careful to avoid provocative roughness in making the arrest in front of the now sizable crowd of students attracted to the scene.

Within a minute about 30 students had seated themselves in front and in back of the police car containing Weinberg and the arresting police officers. In another moment, there were more than 100 students sitting on the ground around the police car, effectively immobilizing it, and their numbers continued to grow.

In Heirich's careful account, "A number of persons claim to have been the first to sit down around the car." He describes the account of Richard Roman, a graduate student in sociology, as typical of a process that many reported going through as they made the sudden decision to defy authority. Roman reports himself as sympathetic to the students but not involved in the controversy at that point. He was crossing the plaza in front of Sproul Hall on the way to a luncheon date when he saw the police arresting Weinberg. He says, "I thought, 'It's a pretty rotten thing for the university to expel and arrest someone.' It made me mad to see the university pulling this trick to punish a few . . ." (1971: 151).

Roman reports that he thought at that moment of a tactic described by civil rights leader Bayard Rustin to deal with a situation in which demonstrators believed that

> . . . the police were moving unfairly against an individual in an effort to intimidate the rest. Rustin would urge the group to confront the police as a unit, so that the latter would have to deal with all of them, rather than with just a few people.
>
> At this point, Roman recalls, he spoke out, suggesting that people step into the path of the police, rather than getting out of the way. He had nothing specific in mind except to refuse to cooperate with this act by the police. After he made this suggestion, he was shoved by "a fraternity type" and got angry.
>
> Roman yelled, "Don't move out of the way!" Shoving, the police pulled Jack Weinberg through the crowd to the car. . . . [Roman] ran toward the front of the car while the police put Weinberg in the car. He began yelling for people to sit down in front of the car, and some obeyed him. He ran around to encourage others to do the same, waving his arms to motion them down. A few other people were also urging others to sit down. For example, he noticed a graduate student, whom he didn't know by name but recognized as being from the same department, encouraging people to sit down behind the car (Heirich, 1971: 151–152).

The police car was held for more than 24 hours while negotiations were carried on by various faculty and student intermediaries. Eventually, the demonstrators released the police car after student representatives and University President Clark Kerr signed a written agreement. The agreement called mainly for a set of procedures for resolving the issues in controversy, including representatives of the protestors as participants in the process. The truce proved temporary, and the conflict built to a climax in which more than 750 people were arrested during the occupation of Sproul Hall.

The organization of the challengers in this encounter contrasts with a critical incident in the growth of the Nation of Islam in Harlem, described by Malcolm X (1965: 236–37). At the time of the incident the organization was "practically unknown" to the general public in Harlem.

Two white policemen, breaking up a street scuffle between some Negroes, ordered other Negro passers-by to "move on!" Of these by-standers, two happened to be Muslim brother Johnson Hinton and another brother of Temple Seven. They didn't scatter and run the way the white cops wanted. Brother Hinton was attacked with nightsticks. His scalp was split open, and a police car came and he was taken to a nearby precinct.

The second brother telephoned our restaurant. And with some tele-phone calls, in less than half an hour about 50 of Temple Seven's men of the Fruit of Islam were standing in rank formation outside the police precinct house.

Other Negroes, curious, came running, and gathered in excitement behind the Muslims. The police, coming to the station house front door, and looking out of the windows, couldn't believe what they saw. I went in, as the minister of Temple Seven, and demanded to see our brother. The police first said he wasn't there. Then they admitted he was, but said I couldn't see him. I said that until he was seen, and we were sure he received proper medical attention, the Muslims would remain where they were.

They were nervous and scared of the gathering crowd outside. When I saw our Brother Hinton, it was all I could do to contain myself. He was only semiconscious. Blood had bathed his head and face and shoulders. I hope I never again have to withstand seeing another case of sheer police brutality like that.

I told the lieutenant in charge, "That man belongs in the hospital." They called an ambulance. When it came and Brother Hinton was taken to Harlem Hospital, we Muslims followed, in loose formation, for about 15 blocks along Lennox Avenue, probably the busiest thoroughfare in Harlem. Negroes who had never seen anything like this were coming out of stores and restaurants and bars and enlarging the crowd following us.

The crowd was big, and angry, behind the Muslims in front of Harlem Hospital. Harlem's black people were long since sick and tired of police brutality. And they never had seen any organization of black men take a firm stand as we were.

A high police official came up to me, saying "Get those people out of there." I told him that our brothers were standing peacefully, disciplined perfectly, and harming no one. He told me those others, behind them, weren't disciplined. I politely told him those others were his problem.

When doctors assured us that Brother Hinton was receiving the best of care, I gave the order and the Muslims slipped away. The other Ne-groes' mood was ugly, but they dispersed also when we left.[3]

---

[3] Malcolm X, *The Autobiography of Malcolm X* (New York: Random House, 1965), pp. 236–37. © by Random House, Inc.

Malcolm goes on to describe how "the *Amsterdam News* made the story headline news, and for the first time the black man, woman, and child in the streets were discussing 'those Muslims.' "

These two encounters cover much of the range in the organization of potential challengers—from spectators at an unplanned public event to "perfectly disciplined brothers" ready to slip away when the orders are given. One shouldn't overlook the degree of organization that exists even among spectators at the events described. Such crowds are typically composed of small clusters of friends and acquaintances (Aveni: 1977). Some of the onlookers in the Harlem crowd may have been members of Temple Seven or friends and relatives of the men of the Fruit of Islam. Similarly, some of the spectators in Sproul Plaza were members of civil rights groups and campus organizations and were clustered in networks of friends and acquaintances. Nevertheless, the contrast in organization is striking.

Organization can be decomposed into *solidarity* and *infrastructure*. The solidarity of a group of potential challengers is a product of both their sense of collective identity and the strength of their interpersonal ties. By *collective identity*, we mean the extent to which potential challengers see themselves as sharing a common fate, affected in the same way by the authority system in which they are operating. Presumably, the passersby at Sproul Plaza shared a sense of being students at Berkeley, but at a large, heterogeneous university, this may not have provided a very strong sense of shared fate.

The Muslims, in contrast, shared both black and Muslim identities—a minority religion in a minority group. Minority status, in general, promotes a strong sense of sharing a common political fate, and in this instance, we have a double dose. The strength of interpersonal ties also differs sharply. We can safely assume that among the crowd in Sproul Plaza there were numerous small clusters of close personal friends, but most people in the crowd were strangers or, at best, distant acquaintances. In the Harlem encounter, in contrast, the Muslims were comrades with intense interpersonal relationships. Indeed, the use of the term *brother* to describe the relationships symbolizes the intense interpersonal bonds promoted by the Nation of Islam.

The organizational advantage of the Muslim challengers was not only in their greater solidarity, but in their infrastructure as well. A group of mutual friends who share a strong sense of collective identity should have high solidarity, but it lacks an important component of organization if the group members have no defined roles within which they can operate. The Fruits of Islam group in the Harlem encounter had more than high solidarity—its members were agents, operating in organizational roles. The internal control that this provided enabled the challengers to operate as a single unit, capable of responding in a collective fashion to contingencies that arose. Lacking such an infra-structure, the Berkeley students perforce had to improvise solutions to organizational problems as they arose. They were forced to handle such delicate affairs as the selection of representatives to negotiate during the very encounter in which they confronted authorities.

Solidarity and infrastructure are subject to change during an en-counter and, indeed, are one major part of micromobilization. But challengers must begin somewhere on these organizational variables, and this starting point is an important determinant of what will happen in the encounter. At one extreme of organization, we find potential challengers who begin as strangers, lacking any sense of collective identity or strong, positive interpersonal bonds to provide solidarity, and lacking an infrastructure that would provide solutions to orga-nizational problems that might arise in the course of the encounter. At the other extreme, we have self-conscious members of a group linked by the strong interpersonal bond of political comradeship, operating in assigned roles.

Assets of challengers can be decomposed into *resources* and *know-how*. By resources, we mean those objects which can be used by the group to achieve its collective goals, and the control of which can be transferred from one person to another. Money, weapons, printing presses, and the like are examples. Different strategies have different resource requirements. To sit down, one needs only one's own body; to engage in a pitched battle with an armed antagonist, one needs some form of weapon.

While resources are of major importance for sustaining long-term challenges, they are frequently not very important in encounters. To be sure, certain actions require a substantial number of bodies. A police car could not be immobilized by two or three people sitting around it. But no special resources are necessary to resist an order to work or to move along. Beyond numbers, none of the encounters described had very heavy resource requirements—one megaphone to address the crowd would probably be sufficient. But it is not hard to imagine other encounters where challengers attempt to oppose the use of force by authorities. Weapons, in particular, are a challenger resource that can-not be ignored in such encounters.

By know-how, we mean knowledge of collective action routines and skill in their application. "At any point in time," Tilly notes, "the repertoire of collective actions available to a population is surprisingly limited. Surprisingly, given the innumerable ways in which people could, in principle, deploy their resources in pursuit of common ends. Surprisingly, given the many ways real groups have pursued their own common ends at one time or another" (1978: 151).

Because many of the Berkeley participants had been active in the civil rights movement and other causes of the early 1960s, going limp when arrested and preventing the police car from moving by sitting around it were part of the repertoire of some of those present. Hence one major asset that potential challengers may possess is the presence of a sufficient number of group members with a good repertoire of collective action techniques, acquired from their experiences prior to the encounter.

Knowledge of what to do is insufficient if the implementation of such knowledge requires skill that members lack. It is not always easy to address a large and unruly crowd and to persuade them of a course of action. It takes some skill to manage an impromptu strike vote or to counter the social control efforts of a smooth and skillful antagonist. In many encounters, participants are confused by the fast-moving flow of events and uncertain of how to deal with them. Again, the presence of a sufficient number of individuals with relevant collective action skills is an important asset that will vary among groups of potential challengers.

Organization and assets of authorities.   There are two sides in encounters with unjust authority, but they are far from symmetrical. The particular authority systems that concern us are bureaucratic organizations. Coleman (1980) calls them complex, disjoint authority systems, and they do not face the same problems that challengers do.

First, Coleman distinguishes between disjoint and conjoint authority relations. The *disjoint case* is one in which subordinates receive an extrinsic reward or benefit in exchange for their compliance. They don't expect that the exercise of authority will especially reflect their interests since there are extrinsic benefits. In the conjoint case, the subordinates receive no extrinsic benefit. Their willingness to comply is based on the expectation that the exercise of authority will reflect their interests.

Coleman uses the illustration of employees vis-a-vis their employer and union. Toward their employer, the authority relation is disjoint—they get paid for the time they put at the employer's disposal. Toward the union, their relation is *conjoint*. They pay it dues, and when they allow the union to act on their behalf and accept its decisions as binding, they expect it to pursue their interests.

Authority systems also may be simple or complex. Here, the distinction rests on whether authority is exercised directly or by a lieutenant or agent. Complex authority systems include the expectation that authority can and will be delegated to designated agents, empowered to act on behalf of the system as a whole.

We assume a disjoint, complex authority system in the encounters we are analyzing. Such authority systems do not face the kind of organizational dilemmas that make collective action so difficult for potential challengers. They have an infrastructure when the encounter begins. When things get too hot for the superintendent in Fisher 1 to handle, he can run to the assistant plant manager. *He*, in turn, can deal with it or size it up as requiring negotiation with the plant manager. Authorities have an established hierarchy of command and a set of well-defined roles already intact. On this side of the encounter, the participants are acting as agents of a larger authority system.

Nor is solidarity much of an issue for authorities except in some extreme cases, considered below. The agents of authority are either employees or conscripts. Loyalty to the authority system may be a useful quality for agents, but authority systems rely on a variety of other inducements and constraints to control their personnel. Those who fail to carry out orders or who mishandle their assignments may be fired or even arrested and imprisoned. Those who carry out their assignments well may be rewarded with promotions, honors, and material benefits.

Normally, then, the organization of authorities is a constant feature not a variable condition of encounters. There are two important exceptions: *dual authority* and *collapsing authority*. In the dual authority situation, there are two (or more) relatively autonomous authority systems represented among the agents of authority present, with the potential of conflict between them. The civil rights movement, for example, produced a number of encounters in which agents of both federal and local authorities were present, operating under independent sets of instructions. Student demonstrators in the 1960s sometimes found themselves confronting agents of more than one law enforcement agency—for example, a county sheriff's department and a city police department.

Such a dual authority situation provides potential challengers with strategic possibilities that are not normally present. Authorities may engage in actions that neutralize or interfere with each other's social control efforts. They may more easily make social control errors—that is, perform acts that are intended to counter the collective action efforts of challengers but that result in enhancing them instead. When dual authority systems are represented, authorities have an organizational vulnerability that they do not ordinarily experience.

An authority system is in crisis and danger of collapse if there is more than a negligible probability that some of its agents may defect to the challengers in the encounter. Normally, this is not an issue. But in revolutionary situations, for example, soldiers given the order to fire on a crowd sometimes turn their weapons on those who issued the orders. In such weakened authority systems, the agents present lack the usual organizational advantage that accrues to authorities and must face many of the same issues that potential challengers typically face. As with dual authority, a collapsing authority system gives this side in the encounter an organizational vulnerability they do not ordinarily experience.

Organization is not usually problematic for authorities, but resources and know-how frequently are. Just as challengers require resources of various sorts for collective action, authorities require resources for social control of would-be challengers. Once participants resist attempts to regulate their behavior in the encounter, the issue of possible sanctions arises.

The ability of the authorities to deliver sanctions differs widely from one encounter to another. At one extreme, we find an isolated agent of authority with little or no ability to summon forth effective sanctions on the spot against those who defy regulation. At the other extreme, we find substantial numbers of armed enforcement agents with reinforcements standing by.

The dynamics of encounters change depending on the immediacy or distance of sanctions for noncompliance. Lining up in front of a police station or surrounding a police car is risky action. One is confronting antagonists with an imminent capability of administering force. Risks are more distant and hypothetical when the agent attempting regulation must transcend the encounter to administer sanctions through calling on other agents at a later time.

The sanctioning ability of authorities requires know-how as well as resources. Just as challengers may bring to the encounter a particular repertoire of collective action techniques, authorities bring a particular repertoire of social control techniques. There are, for example, methods for dispersing crowds such as the one surrounding the police car in Berkeley. Later, the police in Berkeley and elsewhere frequently used tear gas to disperse crowds. Presumably, university officials opposed its use as too provocative on this occasion, and police went along.

In 1964, the handling of such an incident was a relatively new experience for Berkeley police. No doubt, their repertoire of crowd control and dispersal techniques expanded in the years that followed, and similarly, their skill in carrying out these techniques must have increased with experience and analysis of the handling of encounters. Authorities as well as challengers can draw lessons from the mistakes of the past and increase their know-how in future encounters.

The legitimacy of authorities.   The legitimacy of authorities is a matter of the state of mind of potential challengers. They may differ widely in their initial presumption of legitimacy, as the encounters described here reflect.

The Harlem encounter was one extreme. The Muslims of Temple Seven, regarding the white police as an occupying force, complied because it made tactical sense to avoid sanctions, but they felt no obligation to comply. Their protest in this case was directed at police brutality, but they granted little or no legitimacy to the normal, daily operation of the police.

The Berkeley encounter began with somewhat more initial legitimacy. When Weinberg set up a political table in Sproul Plaza, he was self-consciously engaging in an act of civil disobedience against university regulations. Clearly, he felt no initial obligation to honor the authority of Dean Murphy or other university officials whom he would shortly encounter. The initial state of mind was less clear for the many in Sproul Plaza who joined the encounter as it progressed. If a sophisticated political activist such as Roman could describe himself as "not involved in the controversy at that point," one can guess that university officials began with a fairly strong presumption of legitimacy for most participants.

The initial legitimacy was even stronger for workers in the Fisher 1 encounter. No doubt, management was regarded with considerable hostility by many workers, but they came to work for their shift that day accepting the authority of management agents over their work life. Though their resistance focused on the specific exercise of authority represented by the speed-up, an initial presumption of legitimacy operated in the encounter.

Finally, we have the strong and unquestioned legitimacy of authority at the beginning of the Milgram fabrication. The experimenter was presented as a psychologist conducting scientific research at prestigious Yale University. Recognizing the importance of the legitimacy variable, however, Milgram ran a variation in which the authority had more questionable credentials. He created a fictitious organization called Research Associates of Bridgeport, which conducted the experiment in rented offices in a commercial building in the downtown shopping area of Bridgeport, Connecticut. No affiliation with Yale University was revealed until afterward, when subjects were told of the hoax. Milgram found that the rate of compliance with the experimenter's instructions declined somewhat from the baseline runs at Yale, but still remained quite substantial. Clearly, even such fictitious entities as Research Associates of Bridgeport are able to operate on an initial presumption of legitimacy.

The legitimacy of authorities, like the organization of potential challengers, is subject to change in the course of encounters, and this change is a central micromobilization process. The authorities begin the encounter with some initial degree of legitimacy—relatively low in contentious gatherings and relatively high in others where an initial presumption of legitimacy prevails. In the latter type, authorities are safe from rebellion if they act in an ordinary and unexceptionable manner, but they may risk their legitimacy by their actions during the course of the encounter.

PLAN OF THIS BOOK

Resource mobilization theory, we have argued, needs its own social psychology, focusing less on sources of frustration and more on the cognitive and face-to-face interaction processes involved in mobilizing for collective action. This study of micromobilization should focus on encounters, especially on the kind in which potential challengers confront authorities.

We have chosen here to focus on encounters in which the authorities begin with a presumption of legitimacy that is called into question in the course of it. Such encounters are particularly likely to furnish critical incidents and to present a microcosm of long-term mobilization processes.

The centerpiece of our analysis is an encounter with unjust authority that we observed 33 times and recorded on videotape. In it, a group of strangers, hired individually by a company to perform a vaguely defined task, find that the company is acting reprehensibly. They are being asked to perform tasks that will help the company in carrying out its designs. We ask what must happen for the group to mobilize and act collectively against the unjust authority.

The encounter we will analyze is a fabrication. In Chapter 3, we discuss some of the issues, particularly ethical ones, in using fabrications in general and this one in particular. In Chapter 4, we describe an encounter called the "MHRC encounter" in full detail, including its variations, and we explain why it is an especially useful case for studying processes of micromobilization.

In Chapter 5, we discuss the rebellion careers of the 33 groups that we eventually observed. They follow different paths—some leading to successful rebellion, some to partial success, and some to failure. Our major task in this book is to understand the rebellion careers of these groups in a manner that allows us to understand how micromobilization operates in general.

Chapters 6 through 11 analyze these 33 encounters. To insure that our analysis will apply to encounters other than our fabricated one, we illustrate the argument of each chapter with one or more of the critical incidents described above: the Fisher 1 encounter, the Berkeley encounter, and the Harlem encounter. We then apply the argument to our systematic set of observations on the 33 examples of the MHRC encounter.

In Chapter 6, we consider the historical context of encounters. We suggest that this vague concept can be given a more precise meaning and operationalized through the concepts of *climate* and *cleavage structure*. In Chapter 7, we consider the assets of the potential challengers and authorities, especially their know-how. In Chapter 8, we turn to the dynamics of the interaction as we explore the process by which participants learn to work together and develop a collective orientation. In Chapter 9, we consider the process by which potential challengers break the bonds of authority, freeing themselves for unauthorized collective action. In Chapter 10, we examine the process by which participants come to share an injustice frame as a definition of what is happening. Chapter 11 looks at careers as a whole, and examines how prior conditions interact with various mobilizing acts to produce a particular rebellion career.

In the final chapter, we consider the implications of our analysis for a more general theory of micromobilization. We end by discussing the implications of our theory for the practice of rebellion against unjust authority.

Fabrications | 3

TRANSFORMATIONS

Conventions key certain activity as different from the ordinary activity that it resembles. The curtain rises, and we know that we are watching a play about a heresy trial and that the life of the accused is not really in peril. The rehearsal of the play adds an additional lamination—the actors know that, unlike the play where their performance really counts, this time they are only practicing. Goffman (1974) has undertaken the task of analyzing a variety of such transformations with great subtlety.

One main class of transformations is what he calls "technical redoings." The activity being performed is like some identifiable strip of ordinary activity, but all participants, whatever their role, share the understanding that it is being deliberately staged and that the outcomes don't count. A variety of cues alert the participants to the difference between the transformed activity and the ordinary activity to which it is keyed.

Sometimes, an activity is staged so it can be studied. One simulates a real situation to generate or test some hypotheses about how participants in such a situation will act.[1] Natural conditions are simulated as much as possible so that the constructed activity will be as much as possible like the original activity on which it is keyed. Zimbardo et al.

---

[1] The word *simulation* sometimes has the connotation of something fake or inauthentic. We don't mean it in this sense but use it to refer to undeceptive, deliberate redoings of some primary activity—for example, a simulated space flight to aid in the training of astronauts.

(1973: 38), for example, went to considerable lengths to insure verisimilitude in simulating a prison in the psychology building at Stanford University:

> The quiet of a summer morning in Palo Alto, California, was shattered by a screeching squad car siren as police swept through the city picking up college students in a surprise mass arrest. Each suspect was charged with a felony, warned of his constitutional rights, spread-eagled against the car, searched, handcuffed and carted off in the back seat of the squad car to the police station for booking. . . . After a while, [each] was blindfolded and transported to the "Stanford County Prison." Here he began the process of becoming a prisoner—stripped naked, skin-searched, deloused, and issued a uniform, bedding, soap and towel.

All of the participants in Zimbardo's simulated prison knew that they were participating in a simulated prison study. They knew that the prison was scheduled to last for two weeks, and they had volunteered as paid participants for that period. They were not deceived about what to expect but were warned that "as prisoners their privacy and other civil rights would be violated and that they might be subjected to harassment." Although the prison was not created for natural reasons, every attempt was made to make the prison an accurate simulation of an actual prison.[2]

Simulations, then, represent a type of transformation in which all of the participants recognize that the activity is keyed. There is another type—*fabrications*—in which some of the participants are deceived about what is happening. Fabrications are "intentional efforts of one or more individuals to manage activity so that a party of one or more others will be induced to have a false belief about what is going on" (Goffman, 1974: 83). The cues that would alert the unwitting to what is really going on are absent and, indeed, great effort and skill may be required to disguise them.

Participants in a fabrication are in different awareness contexts. For the fabricators—those engaged in managing the performance—it is *transformed* activity. For those who are contained within the fabrication, it is something else—in most cases, primary untransformed activity that has real consequences. To call such a strip a fabrication is to take the point of view of the fabricators.

Fabrications can be benign or exploitive. Benign fabrications claim

---

[2] Zimbardo and his colleagues apparently succeeded too well in this respect. For the inmates in the Stanford University prison, the activity was no longer transformed. They were in fact prisoners for the duration of the simulation, constrained by force from leaving the prison when they wanted to. This could occur only because it continued to be a simulated prison for Zimbardo, his assistants, and the participants serving as guards. When Zimbardo was finally able to recognize that the simulated activity had become real for some of the participants, he called the simulation to a halt.

to be either designed in the interests of the persons contained in them and for their benefit, or in some general interest—such as furthering knowledge—and not against the particular interests of those contained in the fabrication.

As an example of the former claim, consider the surprise party. A person is deceived into thinking that some other, perhaps unpleasant or boring event, will be occurring. She arrives to discover that her friends have conspired to celebrate her birthday. The element of surprise is designed to enhance the pleasure of the occasion for the person contained in the fabrication (and presumably for the fabricators as well).

The presumption of common interest is less clear in cases where the claim is made that a general interest is being served and that the particular interests of the unwitting participants are not being hurt. The example that concerns us here is that of "experimental hoaxing." It is common to mislead subjects in psychological experiments about what is being tested, on the grounds that such knowledge will consciously or unconsciously influence their response. In a full-fledged fabrication, the participants may not even realize that an experiment of some kind is in progress. For them, the primary activity is untransformed.

It is possible, of course, to disagree about how benign a fabrication is. The claim that knowledge will be advanced in an experimental hoax can be evaluated as can the claim that participants are not hurt by it. Evidence can be sought from the participants, and the claims tested empirically. Concerns of this sort are central to our discussion of the ethics of fabrications, but before turning to these ethical considerations, we have some strategic observations about the design of fabrications.

Fabrication technique. Our first attempts at fabrication were clumsy ones. We attempted to create a reality with words, but our participants relied on a variety of contextual cues to decide that what was really going on was a psychological experiment. They were kind to us, however, instructing us on how to improve the fabrication, indicating the cues they used to see through the hoax, and making numerous suggestions to us on how to make our act more convincing.

It turned out, as we no doubt should have known, that they did not put very much weight on our words. They looked at the general setting, and it soon became obvious to us that it would readily occur to people that they were participating in a psychological experiment as long as we conducted our fabrication in a university setting.

They readily spotted small details that were incongruous with the reality that we were fabricating. Length of hair and dress of the fabricators were duly noted, and those of us who appeared in the fabrication learned to conform to the dress code that participants seemed to expect from us. Participants examined the equipment we used, at one point discovering "Property of the University of Michigan" on one piece of it. In response, we developed a series of props to make our staging more convincing in such details.

Experimental design.   The control group in an experimental fabrication consists of a baseline series of iterations run under standardized conditions. One runs a sufficient series to establish stable norms on whatever measures are of interest. Then it is possible to run additional series, varying aspects of the original scenario of theoretical interest and comparing the results with the baseline series.

Our research contained a design of this sort. In the baseline runs, the participants were left to deal with the machinations of unjust authority on their own. In the variations, we provided them with some assistance in the form of different kinds of mobilizing agents. Each type of mobilizing agent embodied a theory of mobilization—that is, he saw to it that certain functions, in theory necessary to produce a successful rebellion career, were performed. Our design called for us to run 20 iterations of the baseline condition and 20 iterations of three different variations for comparison.

In the end, we ran only 33 groups instead of the larger number intended. In midstream, we encountered two groups where the level of stress crossed a threshold that we had not encountered earlier. Our experience with these two groups, both during the fabrication itself and during the dehoaxing period afterward, led us to a decision to stop running additional groups on ethical grounds. There were considerations that led us to feel that, while we were on ethically defensible ground in running the fabrication to the point that we did, we would not have been on very solid ground had we continued.

ON THE ETHICS OF EXPERIMENTAL FABRICATION

We fully accept what Bok (1978) calls the "principle of veracity." Since telling the truth is preferable to lying (unless special considerations are present), the burden of proof must be accepted by those who deceive. This seems especially true when the deception disguises the fact that the primary activity is actually an experiment of some sort. In such fabrications, the participants are fooled into thinking that a transformed activity is something else. The burden of proof would seem to be particularly heavy for those who engage in such hoodwinks.

The first ethical imperative for an experimental hoax is to worry about the welfare of those who will be contained in the fabrication.

One can begin by viewing those who are being deceived as persons who are trying to interpret and understand what is happening in the encounter. Perhaps calling them "participants" rather than "subjects" is little more than a cosmetic change, but it encourages one to look upon the encounter in a different way.

The difference is most clearly reflected in the postfabrication period, commonly called the "debriefing." The use of a single term here blurs the two separate agendas that should be handled in that period. The first agenda is *dehoaxing*, a strip in which the fabricators meet their responsibilities to the participants by explaining to them the nature of the deception and the reasons for it.[3]

The dehoaxing period is an opportunity to test the critical ethical claim that the welfare of the participants has not been hurt and, hopefully, that it has been positively affected by the experience. The participants are in the best position to judge their own welfare. What Milgram writes with respect to his particular fabrication applies generally: "The central moral justification for allowing a procedure of the sort used in my experiment is that it is judged acceptable by those who have taken part in it" (1974: 199).

One can find out in the dehoaxing period whether the participants will support the claim that their welfare has been protected or enhanced. As Bok (1978: 191) observes, "Unfortunately, debriefing does not always succeed. The disappointment may remain; the anxiety or loss of privacy may not be overcome. The experiment may reveal something to subjects about themselves that no debriefing will erase." The dehoaxing period allows for some assessment of how much still seems unresolved for the participants and how much they are willing to give the fabricators ex post facto license for having deceived them.

The second agenda of the postfabrication is debriefing, a strip in which the fabricators, now recast in the role of field workers interacting with informants, attempt to learn more about what the participants were thinking and experiencing while they were contained in the fabrication. One can debrief participants the way one debriefs travelers on what they have learned during their trip.

Debriefing involves asking the participants to help the researchers understand the phenomena that the fabrication is designed to illuminate. It enlists their cooperation in a general purpose embracing all of the participants: the advance of scientific knowledge. To the extent that participants are satisfied that they have not been exploited or

---

[3] Holmes (1976) suggests that part of the dehoaxing obligation involves "desensitizing" the participants, a process of making them feel better about having acted during the fabrication in a manner that they believe to be inappropriate. In many cases of experimental hoaxing, such reassurance would be quite gratuitous since people will be quite comfortable with how they acted.

misused and that some useful purpose is being served, they are likely to be cooperative. Unwillingness on the part of participants to render such assistance is strong evidence against the ethical claims on which the experimental fabrication rests. A successful debriefing depends on earning the goodwill of the participants.

Ex post facto consent is better than no consent at all, but it is less desirable than prior consent. Fabrications raise a particular difficulty for obtaining prior consent since people cannot give it in an informed way without knowing the particulars of the encounter. To reveal such particulars jeopardizes the success of the fabrication in containing the participants. There is, then, a conflict between ethical and strategic considerations.

A reasonable compromise is to obtain prior willingness from people to participate in deception research in general. This is incomplete consent, to be sure, since it is less than fully informed. But this merely underlines the fact that consent is not given once and for all, but needs to be renewed by ex post facto license. Without this renewal, prior consent to be deceived in general provides very little ethical warrant.

LICENSE FOR THE MHRC FABRICATION

In the fabrication used here, a company calling itself the Manufacturers' Human Relations Consultants (MHRC) recruited participants primarily through advertisements in newspapers. A phone number was listed for would-be participants to call. During the recruitment interview, we obtained a degree of prior consent. Among other alternatives, participants were asked whether they were willing to participate "in research in which you will be misled about the true purposes until afterward." Only if they indicated such willingness were they recruited to participate.

We recognized that this prior consent was conditional and not truly informed; hence, it would be necessary to question participants on their ex post facto feelings about the experience. We did this in three ways:

1. During the dehoaxing and debriefing period, we asked participants to fill out a postquestionnaire to record some of their reactions to the encounter. At the end of this questionnaire, we asked: "Now that it's all over, and we have told you what the research is really all about, do you have any misgivings about having participated in this experiment? Please explain."

2. During the dehoaxing discussion, we invited participants to discuss their feelings about various aspects of the encounter, including the issue of our having deceived them. We have not attempted anything systematic with this material, but there is no question that the general

demeanor of the participants during this discussion heavily influenced our judgment about whether they felt injured. If, in the dehoaxing, people seemed generally relaxed and animated, joked and laughed a lot, seemed eager to learn more about what we were doing, and volunteered to assist us in various ways, we took this as evidence that they were not feeling injured and troubled.

3. During the dehoaxing period, participants were asked to sign a sheet with their names and addresses if they were interested in seeing a report of the results. The 146 who left their name and address were sent a short descriptive report of the results from 6 to 12 months after their participation.[4] We also included a one-page follow-up questionnaire on their earlier experience. Participants were again asked about misgivings, but this time we also asked what they felt they had learned from participating, whether they felt exploited, how much stress they experienced, and if they were willing to have the videotape in which they appeared shown to others.[5] Thus we have some evidence on any delayed reactions that might have occurred.

We feared that participants might feel upset and ashamed at having failed to act against the unjust authority we created. We thought we might need to reassure participants that they had acted in an appropriate fashion and had nothing to apologize for. In practice, such reassurance was never needed, perhaps because no group reacted completely passively and quite a few reached very advanced stages of mobilization. Those groups that were relatively passive did not see themselves in that light. In such groups, we were particularly careful to avoid any implication that they had behaved more compliantly than others or than they should have. Generally, participants seemed to feel proud of their actions and the fact that they had personally acted with integrity.

Nevertheless, people might have misgivings for other reasons. They might feel upset about having been taken in by the hoax, or tricked into becoming angry and indignant about an injustice that didn't really exist, or simply at having been put through undue stress. Furthermore, one should be seeking not only the absence of misgivings but some enhancement of the participants' welfare as well. Kelman suggests the principle that "the subject should in some positive way be enriched by the experience, that is, he should come away from it with the feeling that he has learned something, understood something, or grown in some way" (1968, p. 222). Beyond gaining insight, they may have also been entertained and gained materially through being paid for their participation. To what extent did our participants feel misgivings about

---

[4] We began this procedure only after the trial runs were completed, and the signers represent all the participants after this point.

[5] See Appendix A: Questionnaires for the exact wording of the items.

having taken part in the MHRC fabrication, and to what extent did they experience positive benefits?

With the exception of the final two groups that led us to discontinue the fabrication, the dehoaxing and debriefing period was characterized by camaraderie between the fabricators and participants. Many participants seemed interested in the research and curious to learn more about it, and they were uniformly cooperative in filling out our debriefing questionnaire. None of the participants—including those in the final two groups—ever refused to take the additional 10 minutes or so to complete this final task.[6] One might attribute such cooperation to the demand characteristics of psychological experiments. But it is worth pondering the fact that only a few minutes earlier, most of these participants defied demands of the MHRC coordinator.

One might cooperate, of course, while still holding serious misgivings about having participated. Table 3–1 shows the distribution of responses to the debriefing questionnaire item soliciting misgivings. Note that the question did not ask for positive benefits, but many participants apparently felt some welfare enhancement. More than a third both explicitly denied misgivings and *spontaneously* mentioned positive effects.

TABLE 3–1   Misgivings about participation

Response	Percent
No misgivings; positive feelings mentioned	34%
No misgivings; no positive feelings mentioned	52
Ambivalent response	7
Mentions misgivings	7
	100%
Total people involved	170*

* Excludes participants in final two groups.

Of 170 participants, 24 either expressed ambivalence about participating or indicated some reservation or misgiving. Three primary types of reservations were mentioned. Seven people indicated some resentment about having been tricked, although sometimes in quite mild terms. One participant for example, answered, "No [misgivings] (although I don't generally like the idea of people being duped to get

[6] There was one exception, but not on grounds of misgivings. One participant asked to be paid an additional fee for filling out the final questionnaire and also asked to be hired on the project as a mobilizing agent in future runs. We declined both offers.

information). Unfortunately, though I don't like the idea, it's probably the only way to get realistic, therefore meaningful responses." Another wrote, "I still feel a little funny that something was put over on me, but that's how I am with surprise parties and practical jokes, too. It seemed to go well. Good luck!"

Seven others expressed reservations about how they had acted—in all cases, that they had been more compliant than they now felt was appropriate. "The misgivings I have about my actions," wrote one participant, "are only that I didn't verbalize enough of my feelings." Another, who eventually was not compliant, wrote, "A few [misgivings]. Needing money somewhat badly, I was almost willing to compromise."

Seven other participants suggested that the situation was especially stressful for them, although this seemed to produce ambivalence rather than outright objection to having participated. "No [misgivings], I'm physically exhausted and nervous, but in a way I'm glad I did it because I'm a little more certain about my own integrity," one person wrote. "No [misgivings], excepting it's a little hard on the nervous system," wrote another.[7]

Besides these three types of reservations, a few other scattered doubts were raised. A couple of people expressed concern that the results would be used by corporations and government to keep people in line. Another answered yes to the misgivings question, explaining, "I don't believe in the validity of the scientific process. Particularly in the branch known as sociology."

Results from the follow-up questionnaire 6 to 12 months later generally support a picture of very few serious misgivings on the part of participants. Unfortunately, we had only 51 responses from a mailing of 128. While much of this nonresponse came from address changes, those with real misgivings may have been less likely to respond. Among this possibly biased sample, we found only 5 percent expressing reservations. Perhaps more importantly, 90 percent felt that they learned something from participating.

The MHRC encounter did produce a fair amount of stress for participants. The median participant experienced "more stress than one is likely to encounter in an average day," while about 25 percent experienced "more stress than one is likely to encounter in an average month." One person found it "the most stressful experience I have encountered in the last year." For the most part, the amount of stress that participants experienced in the first 31 groups appears to have

---

[7] We don't mean to imply that stress per se is negative. A moderate amount of stress may be conducive to growth and may be responsible, in part, for the enhancement of welfare that more than a third of the participants spontaneously mentioned. But it is possible to get too much.

been moderate rather than severe for the vast majority of participants—about the same as one might expect to find in a classroom game simulation in which participants become emotionally involved.

THE DECISION TO STOP

Given this evidence on the ethical warrant for continuing this research, what led us to stop in midstream without completing our original design? We did so on the basis of new evidence—from two groups in which the stress level appears to have exceeded the moderate amount that we had produced earlier. To put the matter simply, we did not feel comfortable upsetting people to the extent they had been in the last two groups, and we were not confident that our dehoaxing was successful in resolving the tension that we had aroused during the course of the fabrication. Earlier groups typically experienced a lot of release and catharsis during dehoaxing, but some of the participants in these final groups still seemed shaken by the experience.

Our questionnaire evidence supports this. Where only 14 percent of the participants in our earlier groups expressed reservations or ambivalence, 41 percent of the participants in these two groups did so. Furthermore, the misgivings expressed seemed qualitatively different in a few cases than the mild ones expressed earlier. "The monetary compensation wasn't enough to soothe my actual physical nausea. I'm glad to have done it, but I'm really shook, and my blood pressure will be high for hours," one of them wrote. Another wrote, "It's OK to look back now. But the pressure was too much. I've got *the shakes!*"

One participant also had a delayed reaction, calling the next day to say that he had difficulty sleeping following his participation and was still feeling rather shaken. Later, he met with our research group to discuss his reactions, and this discussion further influenced our decision to stop. We, the fabricators, were inevitably affected by the reaction of the participants, especially those of us who actually appeared in the fabrication—that is, the MHRC coordinator and the mobilizing agent. Where earlier we were satisfied that the welfare of the participants was being adequately protected, if not enhanced, now we were in doubt about the validity of this ethical claim.

We might have attempted to reduce the stress that the participants experienced and continued with the fabrication. It turns out, however, that the two groups in question were among the most fully mobilized of any that we had run. As part of this mobilization process, participants became angry and indignant at the actions of the MHRC. The anger was controlled and channeled—not blind rage—but the effort at control may well have increased the stress. Reducing stress, then, would have meant reducing anger toward the MHRC, but controlled anger was part of the very mobilization process that we were studying.

CONCLUSION

The ethical issues in experimental fabrications are far from clear-cut. One may argue, as Warwick (1975) and others have, that there are important cumulative effects of the use of experimental hoaxing. Each new fabrication, however benign it may appear in isolation, adds to the depletion of what Goffman calls "moral reserves." "If you help someone find a contact lens," he writes, "only later to learn that it was all an experiment in bystander apathy, no great psychic stress would seem to be involved during or after the experiment. But the long-term consequences of many such experiments might be that the citizenry will get to feel that any claim upon them had a good chance of being a spoof, and that one is not going to get caught again being generous to someone who is likely to turn out to be a long way from needing it. . . . In brief, willingness to help is a *sacred* thing; to bring it into use for extraneous reasons is to desacrilize it, and ultimately to weaken it."[8]

We are not as quick to bestow sanctity. We grant that the willingness to intervene to help others is highly worthy of respect and is not something to be toyed with frivolously as in the fable of the boy who cried "Wolf!" But it is quite plausible to argue that people who are generous or who resist an unjust authority in experimental hoaxes will feel vindicated and socially reinforced for acting this way and that such tendencies may well be strengthened in the long run by such experiences.

In any event, our decision to stop running the MHRC fabrication did not rest on such general considerations, but on our uncertainties about the degree of stress experienced by some participants in this particular instance. As Gray (1975: 2) puts it, discussing human experimentation in general, ". . . even though certain general principles and guidelines can be widely agreed upon as sound, their application to actual cases will necessarily be interpretive and subjective." In this case, we remain uncertain in our own minds about the wisdom of our decision to stop running the MHRC fabrication in midstream.

There were clear advantages to be gained by continuing. We had completed our set of baseline runs and were pretesting two very interesting variations embodying arguments about what should happen for a group to mobilize effectively against an unjust authority. As it turned out, we have only three examples of each of these variations instead of the 20 intended. With only three, we can be less certain in our interpretations of what happened, and more prone to overrate the importance of factors idiosyncratic to the particular cases. Inevitably, the evidence for some of our arguments will remain ambiguous where it might have been clear-cut.

---

[8] Quoted from personal communication.

On the other hand, we faced the ethical uncertainties produced by our evidence on the last two groups. There was a sense in which the ex post facto reaction of each group to having participated provided the warrant for running the next group. Where one has reasonable doubt about whether one's claim to be protecting the welfare of the participants is valid, this warrant for continuing is in jeopardy.

It's also quite easy for those involved in research of any sort to exaggerate what is to be learned from collecting more data. Counting our usable pretest efforts, baseline runs, and variations, we had a rich array of material on 33 iterations of a highly complex but standardized encounter. There was a great deal to be gleaned from that, and these data were not diminished by the incremental knowledge that we might have gained from completing our original design.

Our arguments about micromobilization are intended to apply to encounters with unjust authority generally, not merely to the MHRC encounter. We hope to show that they are consistent with systematic observations on what happens in this particular encounter. Hopefully, this will increase their plausibility as general hypotheses about the micromobilization process.

These same points would apply if we had carried our original research design to completion. With additional data, we certainly would have revised some of our arguments, arguing more strongly for some parts, and growing more cautious about other parts. But the applicability of the hypotheses to encounters with unjust authority generally would have remained equally problematic.

For better or worse, then, we stopped after 33 iterations of the MHRC fabrication. Henceforth, we will focus on the doughnut without bemoaning the hole as we see what can be learned from the 33 groups who confronted the Manufacturers' Human Relations Consultants.

The MHRC encounter 4

THE BASIC SCENARIO

Imagine that you live in a small- to medium-sized city in southeastern Michigan. One day you happen to be glancing through the classified advertisements in your local newspaper and see a box which says: "PARTICIPATE IN RESEARCH. Market research firm seeks participants for research sessions. EARN $10 in two hours. Call Manufacturers' Human Relations Consultants, (MHRC) 995-0106." You decide to call.

When you call, you are told that the MHRC conducts various kinds of research projects, and you are asked about your willingness to participate in each of the following kinds of research:

Research on brand recognition of commercial products.

Research on product safety.

Research in which you will be misled about the purpose until afterward.

Research involving group discussion of community standards.

You indicate your willingness to participate in the last two types and the recruiter takes down your name and phone number and tells you that the only research project scheduled for the next few weeks involves group discussion of community standards. She offers you various times when groups are being run and, after choosing one, you are instructed to report at the appointed time to a motel near you—a Holiday Inn, for example. You are also called on the evening before and reminded of the engagement.

When you arrive at the appointed time, you see a sign on the hotel announcement board indicating the Manufacturers' Human Relations Consultants (MHRC) and room number. The room you enter has tables arranged in a U-shaped pattern for nine people, with microphones on the tables and three television cameras facing. Various videotaping equipment is also visible. You are addressed by a coordinator, a man in his 20s dressed in a business suit, who introduces himself, checks your name off on his list, and asks you to please take a seat while waiting for others to arrive. He gives you the MHRC introductory letter (Figure 4–1) to read while you wait, asks you to put on a name tag, and exits into an adjoining room.

In a few minutes, he reenters with an assistant and announces that the session is about to begin. He introduces himself and his assistant and asks you to fill out a questionnaire. In the questionnaire, you are asked to express your opinions on a number of issues, including your attitudes toward large oil companies, business practices, employees rights, individuals engaging in sexual affairs, the relative rights of citizens and authorities, trust in the courts and in government in general, interest in public affairs, and willingness to take individual or collective action in various hypothetical situations. You are also asked your age, sex, race, marital status, religion, occupation, education, party affiliation, and organizational memberships.[1]

When you and the others have completed your questionnaires, the coordinator reenters and explains that you will be taking part in a videotaped group discussion about community standards—that is, "standards communities have about what kinds of behavior may be morally wrong." He explains that the MHRC does research to help businesses with their marketing, public relations, and personnel problems and that a client of theirs, a major oil company, is "involved in a dispute with a man who managed one of their local gas stations here in southeastern Michigan." This man is suing the MHRC's oil company client, and the case is coming before a federal court in Detroit.

He explains that the court needs reliable information on just what community standards are and that holding group discussions has been found to be an effective way to get such opinions. The discussions will be recorded on videotape to give the court a good picture of community standards. Participants are being recruited from different walks of life and different communities throughout southeastern Michigan.

Having finished his explanation, he pays you along with other participants and asks you to sign a "participation agreement" (Figure 4–2) in which you acknowledge receipt of payment and awareness of being videotaped.

---

[1] See Appendix A for exact wording of questionnaire items.

FIGURE 4–1   Introductory letter

MHRC   MANUFACTURERS' HUMAN RELATIONS CONSULTANTS

FOSTER TOWER, SUITE 2704, DALLAS, TEXAS 75221

President
PAUL R. BINGHAMTON, JR.

Regional Director
HOWELL GRANT
27 PARKLANE BLDG.
SOUTHFIELD, MICH. 48075   March 26, 1976

Dear Friend:

We of the Manufacturers' Human Relations Consultants would like
to take this opportunity to tell you something about ourselves.
We are a public spirited organization that provides research
services for businesses all over America. Our goal is to help
our clients respond to the changing pattern of American society.
We feel that in this way we can contribute to the continued
strength of the free enterprise system.

We have asked you here today to participate in a study of
community opinion. Some of our clients are involved in court
cases that turn on issues of community standards. We would
like to tell the courts how groups of citizens, such as yourselves, view such standards. So, we are conducting research
with people from all walks of life--businessmen, working people,
students, senior citizens, and housewives.

We are interested in persons who care, persons who understand
the standards of their communities, so that we can help the
courts reach better decisions.

Our interest is great. This is reflected in the compensation we
offer, which is above average for volunteers engaged in such
research. We wish we could offer even more, but we have many
people to reach and only a limited budget.

We offer our sincere thanks to you for assisting in our work.
Your participation will contribute to the business community's
ability to respond in this area of vital social concern.

                              Gratefully,

                              Paul Binghamton

                              Paul R. Binghamton, Jr.

PRB/mjb

The coordinator leaves the pile of signed agreements in sight on a
work table with other materials and asks people to introduce themselves on camera one at a time, stating their name, where they live,
and what kind of work they usually do. He then turns on a videotape
deck[2] and moves in front of the camera, his back to the group, and

---

[2] This deck is actually a prop and is not really recording. The cameras are hooked up
to another tape deck in the adjoining room and this deck remains on throughout the
session.

FIGURE 4–2   Participation agreement

I acknowledge that,

   I participated in a research session conducted by the Manufacturers' Human Relations Consultants on ————————.
   My participation was completely voluntary and I received a
   payment of $————.
   I was aware that this session was being videotaped.
   I understand that any videotapes made are the sole and complete property of the MHRC. Such tapes will not be shown
   for any commercial purpose whatsoever.

   _____
   Signature

   _____
_____

---

announces the project number, date, his name, and that "this board of
citizens is assembled in [X town] under the auspices of the Manufacturers' Human Relations Consultants." You and the other participants
then introduce yourself on camera in turn. When you've completed
this task, the coordinator turns off the deck and presents you with the
following summary of the case you will be discussing, reading it aloud.

   This case is now before the courts. To protect the identity of the
   parties involved, names are not used.
   From June of 1967 until February of 1976 Mr. C. managed a service
   station, holding a franchise from a major oil company. On February 10,
   1976, his franchise was revoked. Mr. C. filed a legal suit against the oil
   company two weeks later.
   The oil company maintains that they terminated Mr. C., only after
   they were convinced that his immoral behavior made him unfit to serve
   as their local representative in his community. This information came
   from a private investigator hired by the company to look into disturbing
   reports about Mr. C.'s lifestyle. Through conversations with Mr. C.'s
   neighbors and landlady, the investigator learned that Mr. C., who is 39,
   was living with a 24-year-old woman to whom he is not married. Although the two of them had shared the same apartment for a year and a
   half, no one had heard them mention any intention of ever getting
   married.
   The company contends that a station manager who represents the
   company must be beyond moral reproach. Their local business depends,
   in part, upon the image that the community has of the local station

manager. But Mr. C. is not living up to the community's moral standards, according to the company, and he would no longer be able to maintain good relations with customers. It is written in Mr. C.'s contract that his franchise may be revoked at any time if he ". . . is no longer fit to represent the company due to arrest, drug addiction, insanity, or similar condition." Moral turpitude is one such 'similar condition,' according to company lawyers. They claim Mr. C. is morally unfit, and the oil company has every right to revoke his franchise.

Mr. C. is suing the company for breach of contract and invasion of privacy. He asserts that his relationship with Miss R. does not affect his competence on the job and is no business of the company. He claims that he was having no problem with customers. According to Mr. C. the oil company was "out to get him" because he criticized the company's gas pricing policies in an interview that appeared on local TV. (An official of the company was later given an opportunity to defend company policies on the same TV station.) It was not until shortly after the TV interview, according to Mr. C., that the company began investigating him.

The oil company, on the other hand, claims that it decided to investigate Mr. C. only after other information had raised doubts about his conduct. Disturbed by this information but unwilling to act on the basis of rumors, the company commissioned a complete investigation. The company contends that it was trying to protect Mr. C. by refusing to act on reports of his immoral lifestyle until they were thoroughly verified. Mr. C.'s TV interview, the company claims, was irrelevant to the investigation of Mr. C. and irrelevant to the subsequent revoking of his franchise.

Having completed the case description, the coordinator presents the group with a card containing the question: "Would you be concerned if you learned that the manager of your local gas station had a lifestyle like Mr. C.'s? Please discuss why you feel the way you do." You are asked to speak up so that the court can get a clear impression of how you feel about the issues and are reminded that you are being videotaped and should speak one at a time. The coordinator explains that he will be watching the discussion on a TV monitor in the next room, turns on the videotape deck, and exits.

After about five minutes of discussion, he comes back in, turns off the tape deck, and distributes the second question: "Would you be reluctant to do business with a person like Mr. C. because of his lifestyle? Please discuss why you feel the way you do." He then designates specific people—about a third of the group—asking them to argue as if they are offended by Mr. C.'s behavior. He turns the tape deck on again as he exits.

The coordinator enters again after five minutes and turns off the tape deck. He indicates that there will be a short break before moving on to the next question and exits for about five minutes, leaving you and the other participants to talk about anything you wish to. At the end of the break, he enters and distributes the third question: "Do you feel that a person like Mr. C. would be bad for your community? Please discuss why you feel the way you do." He designates three additional individuals and asks them to also argue henceforth like members of the community who are offended by Mr. C.'s behavior. Two thirds of the participants have now been so designated. Upon completing these instructions, he turns on the tape deck and exits.

After a five-minute discussion, the coordinator comes back and turns off the tape deck. He indicates that they are having some minor technical difficulties with the videotaping and will need a few minutes for adjustments. When the equipment is ready, he indicates, you will be asked to give a summary statement of your views on the case. Each of you will be asked to speak from the viewpoint of someone offended by Mr. C.'s behavior, saying why it disturbs you, why you don't do business with him, and why you feel he shouldn't have the company's local franchise. He then departs for a few minutes, again leaving you and the other participants with free time to talk.

When he comes back, he indicates that the equipment is all set and he reminds you of the remaining task—to give a summary statement from the standpoint of someone offended by Mr. C.'s behavior. He exits during these statements, turning on the tape deck as he leaves.

When this task is completed, the coordinator reenters, turns off the tape deck, announces that the videotape is completed, and passes out an affidavit (Figure 4–3). "If you'll please sign these, I can notarize them and they'll be official," he says, excusing himself to get his notary seal while you are reading the affidavit.

He returns shortly to collect and notarize the affidavits, thanks everyone for their cooperation, and indicates the session is complete. As you leave the room, you are met by another person who explains that you have been participating in an experimental hoax and hands you an explanatory letter. Everyone is asked to come back for the dehoaxing and debriefing period described in Chapter 3. During the debriefing, you are asked to fill out another questionnaire. This one asks what you were planning to do when you left, what you thought the MHRC wanted from the group, how much you were bothered by various aspects of the encounter, about your past participation in different kinds of collective action (e.g., protest demonstrations), about your thinking about other members of the group and the role they played in the encounter, and about various possible actions that might occur to people in the MHRC situation.[3]

---

[3] See Appendix A for exact wording of questionnaire items.

FIGURE 4–3 Affidavit

Name _____   State _____

Date _____   County _____

City or town _____

I hereby permit the Manufacturers' Human Relations Consultants to utilize video-tapes of a discussion in which I participated on this date. During the discussion I was aware that my comments were being recorded. Further, it is understood that such tapes will be submitted to the United States District Court for the Eastern District of Michigan, Southern Division, in conjunction with an *amicus curiae* brief, and that the tapes will be edited in such a way as to facilitate their presentation to the Court.

_____
Signature

Subscribed and sworn to before me,

this _____ day of _____, 19 _____

_____

Notary Public in and for the
County of _____State of _____

SOCIAL CONTROL STRATEGY OF THE COORDINATOR

The basic scenario described above imagines a completely compliant group. In fact, only one real group ever approximated such compliance. Typically, the coordinator was called upon to deal with a variety of challenges to his authority, both overt and covert, using a social control strategy. By *social control strategy*, we mean the principles governing his handling of such challenges.

Different social control strategies will certainly produce different amounts of compliance. Since we were not concerned with exploring the effectiveness of different strategies, we chose to use a constant strategy of social control. We wished to minimize the issue of sanctions in order to highlight the moral and social-psychological bonds of authority. Operationally, this meant that the coordinator never threatened the participants in any way.

The issue of implicit threat was not completely absent, however. The MHRC was presented as a national corporation representing a major oil company. One might be afraid of having such a company as an enemy. Nevertheless, the coordinator always spoke politely and never suggested to participants there would be disadvantages for them if they did not comply.

Neither did the coordinator offer inducements for compliance, though there may have been implicit inducements in the eyes of some participants. The MHRC had the apparent ability to supply future employment opportunities as a participant in its other research projects. But the coordinator never said anything to suggest there would be future advantages for participants who complied.

The coordinator, with one exception, made no effort to persuade participants that what they were being asked to do made sense on its own terms. He treated participants as if they were agents under his supervision—in effect, temporary employees. The participation agreement which they signed when they received payment in the beginning was treated, in effect, as a contract. The coordinator's social control strategy consisted almost entirely of attempts to activate this commitment.

The coordinator presented himself as an agent of the MHRC, acting under instructions, doing a job about which he felt neutral. Like those he was supervising, he was obliged to perform the task he had been assigned. He tried, as much as possible, to remain calm and matter-of-fact.

In choosing such a social control strategy, we were attempting to minimize the personal confrontation with the coordinator and to maximize the confrontation with the larger authority system, the MHRC. As much as possible, we wanted the coordinator to be responded to as an agent of the MHRC. Participants were confronting a role rather than the particular persons enacting it.

To see how these general principles applied in practice, we will examine the major social control problems with which the coordinator was routinely called upon to deal:

1. Undeclared noncompliance.   Frequently, participants would fail to carry out their assignment to give false opinions without announcing it. They might remain silent, for example, while others talked. Intention is ambiguous in such situations. The coordinator always treated such undeclared noncompliance as unintentional and repeated the instructions again as if they were not understood correctly the first time.

2. Justification for assigning people to give false opinions. If any question was raised at the time of the initial assignment, the coordinator, for the only time, offered a substantive justification of the procedures. He suggested that "it's not much of a discussion when everyone agrees," and that the procedure had been devised to provide a livelier discussion. If the questioning continued, he suggested further that the particular group was not very representative of the larger public, and that it was known that many people in the community felt Mr. C.'s behavior was inappropriate. This was the limit of justification for the coordinator's instructions.

3. Declared noncompliance. The coordinator's first fallback was on the professional expertise of the organization that he represented:

> Look, this is what the research calls for you to do. This project has been designed by professional researchers, and these are the procedures that have been established. My instructions here are quite explicit. This is the way the research is supposed to be done.

If this failed to produce compliance, he invoked their contract with the MHRC for which they had already been paid. Anyone offering to return the money was denied that option:

> Remember, all of you agreed to participate in this project. You've all been paid and you all agreed to cooperate in producing this tape. Now, let's get the job done.

If this failed, he emphasized the full responsibility of the MHRC for the project and the procedures. The meaning of *responsibility* here was that of liability for anything wrong or questionable:

> If, by any chance, there are any problems caused by our procedures, the MHRC assumes full responsibility. Remember, this is *our* project. It's crystal clear that you're only carrying through with the procedures that *we* have established. We are fully responsible. Don't worry about it.

4. Affidavit refusal. When all participants had either complied with presenting false opinions or had explicitly refused to do so, the coordinator moved on to the presentation of the affidavit. Any participants who signed the affidavit were thanked and dismissed.[4] For those who refused to sign the affidavit, there was an additional scene.

---

[4] They were then intercepted in the corridor for early dehoaxing. If any participants walked out during the scenario, they were immediately dehoaxed and invited to join the fabricators in the back room to watch the remainder of the session on television.

The coordinator asked them to wait while he went into the adjoining room to call the company for further instructions on how to deal with the situation. He returned after a couple of minutes and announced that he had checked things with his office. The MHRC would not need the affidavits after all, since the participation agreements signed at the beginning would be sufficient authorization once they were notarized. He proceeded to notarize the participation agreements, placing them on the work table in plain sight. Participants thus had an opportunity to take such direct actions as seizing these participation agreements or the apparent videotape from the session in which they had just appeared.

We hoped to minimize any effects of who played the coordinator role; in fact, three different actors played this part over the course of 33 groups. Two members of the research project were the principal coordinators, covering 30 groups between them. We had the comfort of knowing that rebellion career was not affected in any obvious way by differences in who played this role. The proportion of "successful" groups was about the same for the two main coordinators. While there were subtle differences—for example, in how rapidly each would exit after giving instructions to the participants—we have not been able to uncover any evidence that the processes we are studying were affected in some systematic way by differences in coordinator style.

SOME ADVANTAGES OF THE MHRC ENCOUNTER

The MHRC encounter was one special case of encounters with unjust authority with its own idiosyncratic characteristics. To understand why it is an especially useful case for studying micromobilization, we return to our earlier discussion of contrasts among encounters.

1. The sanctioning ability of authorities.   We argued in Chapter 2 that the most important asset of authorities is the immediate availability of sanctions. Clearly, a great deal of compliance can be accounted for by inducements and constraints. We accepted this and did not attempt to explore the relationship between the sanctioning ability of authorities and rebellion career in this encounter. By deliberately minimizing the issue as a reason for compliance, we maximized the possibility of learning about the moral and social-psychological bonds that hold participants in authority systems—and about how such bonds are broken.

2. The organization of potential challengers.   We argued in Chapter 2 for the importance of prior organization among the challengers. In the MHRC encounter, the potential challengers were strangers to each other. More highly organized challengers have already solved many of the problems that a group of strangers must face in taking collective action. By choosing unorganized challengers, however, we maximized the possibility of learning about nascent organization, and of studying organization as an emerging process. Clearly, we will have less to say about the kinds of problems that emerge in later stages of organization than we will about the beginning of the process.

3. *Relative complexity of the scenario.* The MHRC scenario was not a simple one, and it was easy for participants to be confused about what was really going on. Although an injustice frame may seem obvious to a reader who is aware of the whole scenario and the intention of the research, it required a good deal of interpretation by the participants who were in the midst of it. It took time for the injustice frame to develop and spread among the group and, in some groups, participants remained uncertain and tentative about what was happening even as late as the affidavit scene.

If micromobilization is to be studied as an unfolding process, it must develop gradually enough to enable us to decompose its elements. It is easy to imagine a scenario in which matters would come to a head much more rapidly. One could hook puppies to electrodes and convince people that they were giving such lovable creatures painful electric shocks, then convince them further that data from this research were being purchased by an unnamed foreign government for use in interrogating political prisoners. The pace of action in such a scenario might well telescope the processes of interest into a few brief moments. The MHRC scenario, in contrast, had a series of scenes in which the action could build to a climax or fizzle as the coordinator presented participants with a continuing series of dilemmas of compliance.

We wanted significant variation in the rebellion careers of our groups. It is this variation that we hoped to explain, and it would not have served our purpose had our scenario produced a uniform response. The MHRC encounter produced several important kinds of rebellion careers, and accounting for their differences in theoretical terms was an ample challenge.

We wanted to find a specific example of a generic case that would resonate for a heterogeneous group of participants. The generic case was that of an individual fighting back against a powerful and devious corporation. This is an important cultural motif, cutting across major societal cleavages of social class, race, ethnicity, and gender. Coleman (1974) argues for the universalism of a particular kind of loss of power in contemporary society. All of us real people have been losing power to corporate persons, including both private and public organizations.

If so, the plight of Mr. C. should have struck a sympathetic chord for a very wide range of people. Our participants were mixed in social class, education, occupation, race, age, gender, and ethnicity. Our scenario was contingent on such a mixed group reaching consensus fairly easily. The case of Mr. C. worked well in this regard. It was credible to the people, and no group failed to reach consensus on the question: "Would you be concerned if you learned that the manager of your local gas station had a lifestyle like Mr. C.'s?"[5] Of course, to move from such shared sympathies to collective action against the MHRC was a long road with many pitfalls; only some groups made it to the end.

VARIATIONS

Since not all of our 33 groups were run under identical conditions, it is useful to distinguish three categories among them: trial runs, baseline runs, and systematic variations. The basic scenario describes the 18 groups that we call baseline runs. Six of our groups were systematic variations of the basic scenario, alike in all respects except for the introduction of a mobilizing agent. Two different versions of a mobilizing agent were contained in this set, each with three iterations.

Writing a part for a mobilizing agent puts theory into practice. The theory suggests that certain functions must be performed and certain problems solved or the rebellion career will fall short in some important way. The mobilizing agent's part does not call upon him to act until *after* there is an opportunity for other participants to perform his functions spontaneously.

The exemplar variation.   The mobilizing agent in this variation sets an example for the group. Participants witness the fact that at least one of their members is growing increasingly disturbed about what is happening. The thing that is happening is shared—that is, the conditions that are producing the anger are common conditions. The exemplar is a reasonable person, not simply someone quick to get upset. He expresses his concern publicly and acts on it. This puts others in the position of having to choose, through their individual actions, whether to support the authorities or the rebels. The exemplar makes certain that participants have this choice if it is not offered spontaneously by the actions of other participants.

The mobilizing agent in the exemplar variation is *not* an organizer. He makes no effort to enlist the support of others, although he welcomes it when it is offered spontaneously. To see how this role operates concretely, we will review the exemplar's actions over the course of the scenario.

On arriving he was agreeable but reserved and didn't introduce any

---

[5] There were a few groups in which a minority were concerned and expressed disapproval of Mr. C.'s lifestyle, but no one claimed that this provided sufficient grounds for firing him.

topic of conversation. He responded and discussed whatever topics were introduced by others, being careful to remain agreeable, making polite small talk at a pace initiated by others. Throughout the instructions, he was compliant.

During the first and second question, he expressed standard views favorable to Mr. C.'s side of the case. At that point, if no one had already made such a challenge, he told the coordinator, "Since the oil company is planning to use this in court against Mr. C., I don't think you should be telling us what to say." Note that he had not himself been asked to argue as if he were offended by Mr. C.'s behavior, so he had not personally faced the issue of complicity yet.

This issue arose only near the end of the discussion scenes, when everyone in the group was asked to give a summary statement against Mr. C. At that point, the exemplar publicly and unequivocally refused to comply. He also refused publicly to sign the affidavit that the coordinator subsequently presented. During the latter scene, he declared his opposition to the project as a whole, declaring that it "should be investigated, exposed, and stopped," but he left it to others to worry about how this could be accomplished.

As scripted, our exemplar was a bit on the slow side for actual groups in the three iterations that we tried. Others were constantly beating him to the punch, and he turned out to be considerably less of an example than others whom he ended up supporting in these groups. A viewer would have been hard put to distinguish the three exemplar variations from many of the baseline runs or to recognize our scripted exemplar as a major protagonist.

The organizer variation. The mobilizing agent in the organizer variation focused on the group's capacity for acting collectively. More specifically, he was responsible for the following functions:

Orienting the actors toward a recognition of group consensus.

Leading the group toward a shared definition that MHRC behavior is improper.

Providing procedural suggestions that would help the group to develop an apparatus for acting collectively.

Helping the group to identify a repertoire of specific collective actions that might be taken to remedy the situation.

In the organizer variation, the mobilizing agent did not challenge the coordinator at any time. He always supported acts of resistance or opposition by others but never initiated such action. He never resisted coordinator instructions unless at least one other person had already resisted the same instruction.

During the arrival and introduction, his part was identical to the exemplar's. His one additional task in the early scenes required that he make sure others recognized a consensus on the case, thereby making the consensus public and explicit.

During the first break, the organizer directed the discussion to the MHRC procedures by asking for opinions about them. During the second break, he directed discussion to whether or not the group should do what was being asked of them, suggesting that they should decide how to act as a group. He was not the first to resist, but if someone else refused to give opinions unfavorable to Mr. C., he refused also.

After people had read the affidavit, he suggested that all of them refuse to sign. During these last scenes, he also urged that they take some further action against the MHRC, soliciting suggestions from group members. If group members pursued such suggestions for further action, he raised the question of procedures, asking how and when they could get together to take further steps.

The organizer performed one other important function—he attempted to prevent individuals from walking out, urging them to stay so they could all take appropriate action together. If a group decided to walk out collectively, however, he had instructions to support such action and to walk out with them.

As scripted, our organizer's role was frequently preempted in part by other members of the group. Again, he was not a very conspicuous actor in the three actual iterations. There were, however, certain critical moments when the organizer contributed something quite specific that may have altered the course of at least one group's rebellion career in an important way—but this takes us ahead of our story.

Trial runs.   Nine of our groups were run before the baseline series. Since we regarded these, at the time, as pretest runs, we were regularly altering aspects of our basic scenario to improve it. The trial runs differed from each other and from the baseline series in a number of important respects, rendering interpretation and comparison more difficult. Given our unexpectedly attentuated data set, we included these groups in our analysis, but we will necessarily need to distinguish them at some points from their more standardized cousins. Specifically, they varied from the baseline runs in the following major ways:

1. Of the nine groups, five contained a mobilizing agent. This mobilizing agent was not instructed in the more controlled way of the exemplar and organizer variations but was allowed to respond more spontaneously, trying whatever might seem to work.
2. The coordinator's social control strategy was not fully developed. In many groups it was similar to the one appearing in the baseline

scenario, but the coordinator's role was much less clearly defined and his behavior more variable.
3. The specific case varied. In one version, for example, the victim was a Ms. C., who had been fired as the assistant personnel manager of a large company, allegedly for her lifestyle but apparently for her union-organizing activities.
4. Six trial runs were held in Ann Arbor with students. Most of the baseline runs, in contrast, were held outside of Ann Arbor, and the students participating in such runs were always a minority.
5. In some of the runs, participants discovered the hoax before the end. When this happened, we began the dehoaxing and debriefing immediately, making the scenario less complete than the others.
6. Participants were typically paid only $5 to $7 instead of the $10 paid in the baseline runs.

The trial runs were a hodgepodge. Nevertheless, there were several quite interesting rebellion careers represented among them; with proper care, we can learn from them also.

NATURE OF THE SAMPLE

All in all, some 260 people participated in one or another version of the MHRC encounter. Who were these participants, and how representative were they of the population as a whole? The answer is that they were a great deal more heterogeneous than a population of college students, but clearly not as representative as an equal probability sample of adults in the Detroit area. They were people with the time and inclination to spend two hours in the day or evening participating in research.

We did not expect our sample to represent the adult population, but we wished it to include a broad range of people. We hoped, in this fashion, to ensure that the processes we were studying were robust enough to appear in heterogeneous groups and that what we witnessed was not dependent on the peculiarities of the student subculture, for example. A look at the social background characteristics of our participants gives some sense of how successful we were in this regard.

Our information on the participants comes from the beginning questionnaire, an instrument that we didn't introduce until the last three trial runs. The first six trial runs are excluded from Table 4–1, but the missing cases are almost entirely graduate and undergraduate students at the University of Michigan. Even without these cases, the participants tended to be quite young, with a median age of 24 and a range from 18 to 62. While there were a handful in their 50s and 60s, only 17 percent were over 30. Slightly more than half of the participants were women, and 10 percent of them were black or members of other racial minorities. Less than one-third of them were married at the time.

They were quite variable in religious preference and occupation. Only 20 percent were full-time students; another 8 percent were enrolled in school part-time while holding a job. Some 63 percent held a regular job. Only 20 percent had not gone beyond high school; the median educational level included some college. Slightly more than a third were college graduates. Less than one fifth were union members.

TABLE 4–1 Background characteristics of participants

Characteristic	Percent
Age:	
18–21	28%
22–25	33
26–29	22
30 or over	17
Total	100%
Sex:	
Male	45
Female	55
Total	100%
Education:	
High school graduate or less	20
Some college	44
College graduate	17
Postgraduate	18
Total	99%
Employment:	
Regular job	63
Full-time student	20
Employed student	8
Nonworking homemaker	7
Unemployed	2
Total	100%

In attempting to explain rebellion careers, we will examine the extent to which the composition of the group accounted for what happened in the encounter. For now, we can conclude that our participants were quite heterogeneous even though they tended to be younger, more highly educated, and more middle class than a cross-section of the adult population.

58

SUMMARY

We have tried to convey the basic MHRC encounter and its variations in the most concrete form, to convey the encounter as one might have experienced it as a participant. The action in our scenario unfolded gradually, increasing the visibility of the processes we wished to study. By minimizing the sanctioning ability of the coordinator, the encounter highlighted the social psychological and moral bonds that hold people in role in authority systems. By using strangers without prior organization as potential challengers, the encounter highlighted the emergence of social movement organization. By introducing complexity about what is happening, the encounter highlighted the process by which an injustice frame develops and becomes shared. Finally, the MHRC encounter produced a rich and varied set of rebellion careers, and we turn now to their examination.

Rebellion careers | 5

DILEMMAS OF COMPLIANCE

All our groups began their life in the same way. They started off compliantly enough, accepting the coordinator's regulation of their behavior and settling into the assigned tasks without difficulty. Everyone completed the questionnaire cooperatively, introduced themselves on camera as asked, and began a discussion of the cases as asked. Except in one group, everyone signed the participation agreement, acknowledging that they were willingly videotaped, received payment, and that the tape produced was the sole property of the MHRC. The resisting group followed the lead of a retired book editor from a local publishing house who suggested that he never signed anything in advance. The exchange was polite and reasonable, but this unusual response foreshadowed later fireworks. Even this group complied willingly enough with the remainder of the coordinator's benign instructions. At the conclusion of their first discussion of the case of Mr. C., all groups were cooperating with the coordinator. None exhibited any readiness for collective action against the MHRC.

It is useful to think of each group as having a rebellion career. The first discussion of the case of Mr. C. was an early point, a prologue, in the brief life span of a rebellion career. As the MHRC scenario unfolded, participants faced efforts by the coordinator to gain their increasing complicity in helping the oil company prosper in its legal battle with Mr. C. Each new effort confronted the potential challengers with an additional dilemma of compliance. To describe rebellion careers more systematically, we have divided the critical part of the MHRC scenario into three acts.

In act 1, the coordinator makes his first effort to gain recorded opinions critical of Mr. C.'s behavior. Until this point, complicity has been implicit. Some participants have already expressed uneasiness and discomfort about helping the MHRC, but there has been little or no reason to reject any of the specific directions given by the coordinator. Now an attempt at gaining more active complicity is being made, and the participants must respond in some fashion, individually or collectively. Their response to this initial dilemma of compliance, and the ensuing interaction with the coordinator and discussion of the case, comprise the first act.

In act 2, the degree of complicity is steadily increased in a series of scenes, punctuated by two breaks in the action when participants may talk to each other, undistracted by any instructions from the coordinator. The act builds to a final scene in which all participants are asked to act complicitly.

In act 3, the coordinator introduces the affidavit in which participants grant their permission to use and edit the videotapes. Depending on what happens, it may include the final scene in which the coordinator announces the MHRC's intention to use the tapes anyway, without needing further permission from the participants.

A group's readiness for collective action opposing the MHRC shifted over time. Initially, the participants were unmobilized—their readiness for collective action was nil. Every group had a particular history of changes in readiness, made visible through how participants responded to the dilemmas of compliance. A group's rebellion career, then, is its characteristic set of responses to the dilemmas it confronts during its life span.

COMPLIANCE RELEVANT ACTIONS

There are, of course, as many careers as there are groups, and our first task is to reduce this complexity by identifying recurrent patterns—essentially a typology of rebellion careers. In the MHRC encounter or any other encounter with unjust authority, group members engage in a variety of actions in responding to dilemmas of compliance. We distinguish seven broad categories of relevant actions:

1. *Compliance.* Participants attempt to carry out the requests of authorities to the best of their ability, frequently attempting to demonstrate their competence in the process. They may ask questions of the authorities, but these are designed to clarify their instructions rather than to elicit justifications of what the authorities are asking.

In the MHRC encounter, we considered that participants were acting compliantly when they filled out the questionnaire, introduced themselves as requested, signed what they were asked to sign, and discussed the case in a manner consistent with the coordinator's instructions.

2. Evasion. From *The Good Soldier Schweik* by Jaroslav Hasek:

Officer: I've already told you to hold your tongue. Did you hear?

Private Schweik: Beg to report, sir, I heard you say I was to hold my tongue.

Officer: Himmelherrgott, hold your tongue then. When I say the word, you know full well we don't want any of your lip.

Private Schweik: Beg to report, sir, I know you don't want any of my lip.

Participants acting evasively do not confront the authorities directly, but neither do they perform in the correct or desired manner. Like the Good Soldier Schweik, they are apparently compliant, but in practice, their performance is marred by error from the standpoint of authorities. They attempt to avoid surveillance so that a confrontation can be avoided. Any failure to comply is implicit and not openly acknowledged by the participants.

In the MHRC encounter, participants developed a number of skillful evasion techniques. We considered all of the following to be examples of attempted evasion:

Some participants remaining silent when asked to give opinions unfavorable to Mr. C., but without giving any indication that they did not intend to comply.

Some participants speaking as if they were a representative of the company rather than as a member of the community offended by Mr. C.'s behavior.

Some participants sharing their unfavorable opinions in an exaggerated or sarcastic way. In one group, for example, a participant doing his best to sound like Gabby Hayes intoned, "Next to ma waaf, ma car is ma favritt thang, an' ah ain't sending neither of 'em tuh thet gas stoishen."

Some participants prefacing their compliant remarks with declarations that they were not giving their real opinions.

3. Rim talk. Every strip of ongoing activity has a larger context in which it is embedded, and using Goffman's term, we call this surrounding context the *rim*. Participants, while they are engaged in the activity, usually take the rim for granted. Students participating in a classroom discussion are focused not on the unspoken rules governing the classroom setting but on the content of the course. Perhaps the instructor is late in arriving, and this event turns their attention to the rim. They may then discuss how long one should wait for the instructor to arrive before leaving and whether a professor deserves more consideration than a mere teaching fellow. *Rim talk* refers to such discussion of the setting of ongoing activity.

In encounters with authority, rim talk has a special meaning: it involves some implicit or explicit questioning of the authorities' conduct. Participants may argue with attempts at regulation and push the authorities to justify their requests. They may attempt to set conditions, making their cooperation a matter of negotiation rather than something to be taken for granted.

In the MHRC encounter, we treated the following acts as rim talk:

Requests for justification. Some participants asked, "If you want to get public opinion, why are you telling some people to give opinions that they don't really believe?"

Negotiating conditions of compliance. Some participants asked the coordinator for assurances or guarantees: "Can you assure us that the court is going to know these aren't our real opinions?" or "Will we be able to see the tape after it is edited?"

4. Dissent. Participants publicly object to the way authorities are acting. Participants criticize or express disapproval of the authorities or their behavior and verbally reject their justifications. This disapproval may be expressed with varying degrees of intensity and explictness. In the MHRC encounter, we found all of the following:

Polite demurrers: "It doesn't seem right that you're asking us to argue only one side of the case."

Accusations of bad faith: "Do these professional people know that what you're in fact doing is suborning perjury?"

Denunciations and insults: "This, ladies and gentlemen, is what Watergate is all about."

5. Resistance. Participants openly refuse to do what the authorities ask them to do. Unlike evasion, noncompliance is openly acknowledged. Whereas evasion involves slyly botching the requested performance, resistance involves overt refusal to perform.

Acknowledgment of noncompliance forces authorities to respond in some fashion. They may explicitly ratify the noncompliance by withdrawing the request or implicitly ratify it by making no effort to enforce or repeat the request. Usually, however, participants who sustain resistance to authorities must withstand the pressing of demands for compliance. In the MHRC encounter, resistance took various forms, some of it polite and some of it defiant:

Some participants announced that they would not present opinions that they did not hold.

Some participants ripped the affidavit into pieces or crumpled it in a ball and threw it on the floor at the coordinator's feet.

Some participants shouted their refusal. "No way!" yelled one participant upon reading the affidavit.

Some participants gave apologetic refusals. "I can't sign this. I'm sorry," was a typical example.

Some participants made their resistance final by walking out.

6. *Direct action.* Participants in the encounter attempt to sabotage the authority system on the present occasion. Direct action involves an attack, during the encounter, on the person or property of the authorities—an attack aimed at obstructing or impeding the operation of the system in some way. Sitting down around the police car in Berkeley is an example.

In the MHRC encounter, participants publicly considered two kinds of direct action, and actually engaged in one:

Some seized the participation agreements they had signed early in the session, after the coordinator announced the agreements would be used in lieu of the unsigned affidavits.

Some participants discussed seizing the videotape of their discussion, but none actually did so.

7. *Preparation for future action.* Participants act to increase their readiness for later collective action. Readiness for future action is a matter of both intention and capability, and our criteria focus on both. With respect to intent, participants may suggest future actions to other potential challengers and attempt to gain their support for them. Hence they use the present encounter to begin the planning of further action. With respect to capability, participants may consider the logistical and communication problems of future action, including their ability to reassemble after the encounter. Before breaking up, they may set a time and place for a future gathering.

In the MHRC encounter, the following actions were included as preparation for future action:

Whistle blowing. Discussion of future action typically focused on the public exposure of the MHRC and its shenanigans. Such discussion was frequently accompanied by the gathering of evidence. Participants took the MHRC's introductory letter, for example, folded it carefully and put it in a pocket or purse.

The particular form of exposure varied, with groups exploring such possibilities as going to a newspaper, consulting a lawyer, calling the procedures to the attention of judicial authorities, the Better Business Bureau, or other public officials. For our purpose, we ignored such differences, focusing on the intention to conduct some further investigation as the criterion. The following exchange from one of our groups provides an example of intended whistle blowing:

Jack: [*gathering materials from the table and folding them up*] I'm going to take these things over to the *News* right afterward. I'm going to talk to an editor.

Leif: Have them publish something about this, so they don't sucker more people into it.

Chuck: Go to the *News!* Go to the *News!*

Roberta: Can we all go to the *News* together?

Jack: Oh, sure.

Leif: Yeah, it's probably a good idea, so they know . . .

Dealing with logistics. If participants were to act as a group in pursuing an investigation of the MHRC, they had to take a few steps involving their capacity to reassemble. All of the following were considered acts that dealt with the logistics of future action: the planning of a meeting at some other place, the exchanging of addresses and phone numbers, and the employment of some division of labor for the performance of future tasks (for example, one person calling a lawyer, another person calling the newspapers).

For some purposes, we will combine those forms of action that go beyond evasion and rim talk. We use the term *protest actions* to refer to the more advanced forms of noncompliance—that is dissent, resistance, direct action, and preparation for future action.

SUCCESSFUL CAREERS

Act 3, with the presentation of the affidavit, was the climactic test for potential challengers in the MHRC encounter. A group able to get everyone to refuse to sign achieved a major benchmark of success in its rebellion career, and we use this as our major outcome measure in describing careers.

Unanimous resistance has some ambiguity as collective action because it can represent nothing more than each individual deciding independently to resist. There is much reason to think that, in the MHRC encounter, something more collective was happening than individuals acting independently but in unison. First, the resistance was always discussed publicly and it became the focus of the interaction. Second, there was considerable evidence that the challengers succeeded in defining resistance to the affidavit as a group norm to which the uncertain and wavering felt pressure to conform. Some, who had already signed, crossed their names out or tore up the form. Overt attempts to influence are frequently made on waverers in such groups, and signers must be prepared to accept some public scorn from other participants.

Sixteen of our 33 groups achieved collective resistance, a successful rebellion career benchmark. Nine of the successful groups met a second criterion in addition—they prepared for future action. Of these nine *mobilized* groups, five met a third criterion as well: they engaged in the direct action of seizing all or most of the participation agreements.[1]

Not all successful groups followed the same career. We distinguished two important subtypes by their response to the initial dilemma of compliance in act 1. Seven of the groups were *quick starters,* who confronted the coordinator almost immediately.[2] Indeed, two of these groups were ultra quick starters in which resistance became so general in act 1 that the coordinator was forced to depart from the script, abandoning most of the second act and moving rather quickly to the affidavit scene with the rather lame claim, "Well, I guess we have enough good material." Here is a scene from one of these ultra quick starters:

Coordinator: [*enters the room, turns off the tape deck, and approaches the group*] That was fairly lively there, and I think we can move on to the second question. But for this question, we're going to make an adjustment in the procedure here. What we're going to do on this question is, we're going to ask Dick and Linda and Jean to take the point of view of someone in the community who's offended by Mr. C.'s behavior.

Carl: Would you mind leaving the tape on while you say this?

Coordinator: Well, this is standard procedure here.

Carl: Would you mind leaving the tape on while you give us these instructions, so that it doesn't appear . . .

Coordinator: That's not what my instructions call for me to do. That would be, I guess, a waste of tape. But I certainly . . . I just follow the instructions.

Carl: [*incredulously*] You're telling somebody to pretend, and you're getting a

---

[1] There were some important design problems that made either preparation for future action or direct action less than ideal as a measure of a successful rebellion career in the MHRC encounter. First, in a few groups in the trial runs, participants saw through the fabrication during the affidavit scene and aborted the scenario before direct action became fully relevant or they had sufficient opportunity to discuss any possible next steps. Second, and more important, many participants felt inhibited about discussing their plans under the eye of the camera, with the coordinator hovering offstage. They knew they were being monitored, and even if they were in such a rebellious state that they had little concern for what this MHRC flunky might think, he was still a potential spy who could report on their actions to his superiors. Under the circumstances, participants sometimes resorted to whispers that we were unable to monitor or, as a group, covered the microphones with plastic cups that prevented our hearing their discussion. Perhaps participants would have begun such future-oriented action as soon as they left, but our dehoaxing procedure prevented this outcome; or perhaps more of it went on beforehand than we were able to detect. Third, our design was flawed in not requiring that direct action or future action be collective to be effective. It doesn't require a group to call a newspaper, although it undoubtedly helps to have moral support. It doesn't require a group to seize the participation agreements. For all of the above reasons, collective resistance to the affidavit makes the cleanest and most reliable measure of success in the MHRC encounter even though the other outcome measures are theoretically as important.

[2] More precisely, quick starters are defined as successful groups in which, during act 1, a third or more of the participants take some protest action—that is, dissent or resist.

videotape of them pretending, but you're not putting on the tape that you're telling them to pretend?

Coordinator: If you noticed what happened here in this first discussion, it was largely the case that most people were on the same side. And we found in the past that you can get a much more lively—and fuller—discussion if there are some differences of opinion within the group. And so we're asking these three people to take the point of view of someone who's offended by Mr. C.'s behavior, so we can get a livelier discussion.

[Several group members stiffen during the coordinator's speech and Linda and Frank exchange looks of disbelief. Frank looks away and slowly shakes his head while Linda stares at the coordinator, her mouth agape. Several murmurings are heard as the coordinator finishes.]

Frank: But that's not the point that they . . .

Linda: [*loudly*] I don't feel that way. If I don't feel that way, I'm not going to act like I do! Especially on the tape!

Coordinator: Well, no, it's not . . . now, it, it, it's really . . . I'm sure you'll find that it's first quality. It's much easier to do when you make an effort to just sit and think for a minute . . .

Linda: [*looking at Carl*] I'm not going to act in some way I don't feel.

Coordinator: There are people like that in the world who feel that way, and we're asking you to act as if you feel that way.

[Linda looks away, shaking her head. Other members sit silently, eyeing the coordinator.]

Coordinator: And you'll see, if you try that, how much livelier the discussion gets, and how much better this whole thing will work then. So let me ask you to try that, OK? And we can move into the second question, and if you three people will take the point of view of someone offended by Mr. C.'s behavior . . . [*leaves the room, turning on the tape deck as he exits.*]

Rebecca: [*triumphantly*] This, ladies and gentlemen, is what Watergate is all about!

[The group roars with laughter.]

Linda: I'm not going to say anything.

Frank: [*barely audible*] I mean, I'll take the money, but this is the most ludicrous afternoon . . .

Rebecca: I think we should object on principle.

Randy: I know one thing, it's against my personal thing to try to, uh, go against my own ideas.

The five quick-starter groups that reached a full second act responded variably through these scenes. Typically, they reached a temporary modus vivendi with the coordinator, but dissent and resistance flared up at different points. Note that the coordinator was instructed to correct attempts at evasion but, in practice, he was frequently unsuccessful. If many people were practicing evasion and the coordinator had already made some effort to correct it, there was little he could do other than challenge the most blatant evasions. By the end of the second act, the coordinator was usually quite grateful for such half-compliant statements as

> Well, I feel that if, um, you're a public servant and you're working for a company, that you're in the public eye all the time. Then I suppose that you do have the obligation to uphold certain standards. But I also do not agree with violation of private rights. I want that made clear.

It might be said of the quick-starter groups during the second act that they felt they had made their point. An uneasy truce prevailed, punctuated by bursts of dissent and resistance. Evasion attempts were common and frequently successful, typically reaching a point at which the coordinator was forced to settle for what he had and move ahead to the final act.

The other nine successful groups were *late bloomers*. They differed most sharply from the quick starters in act 1, where they were relatively compliant. Dissent or resistance began to surface in act 2 for most of these groups, although two ultra-late bloomers were still generally compliant in the scene in which final summary statements critical of Mr. C. were requested.

Neither type monopolized direct action or preparation for future action. Quick starters were slightly more likely to seize the participation agreements (43 percent versus 22 percent for the late bloomers), but late bloomers were slightly more likely to prepare for future action (67 percent versus 43 percent for the quick starters). These differences are not statistically significant, and we make no effort to interpret them. Table 5–1 summarizes our description of successful rebellion careers.

OTHER CAREERS

It is useful to think of potential challengers who have become actively rebellious as a membership group that others may join or

TABLE 5–1 Successful rebellion careers

Label	Number	Collective resistance	Preparation for future action	Direct action	Act 1 protest
			Criteria		
Successful groups	16	Yes	?	?	?
Mobilized groups	9	Yes	Yes	?	?
Fully mobilized groups	5	Yes	Yes	Yes	?
Quick starters	7	Yes	?	?	Yes
Late bloomers	9	Yes	?	?	No

quit. When a subgroup is resisting and a new person joins in, the challenging group has grown; if someone who was previously resisting starts complying, the challenger has shrunk.

To be considered a member of the challenging group in the MHRC encounter, a participant had to engage in some act of dissent or resistance. Membership then remained in effect unless the person publicly advocated compliance with the coordinator's instructions—clear evidence of defection. In successful groups, the challenging group encompassed 100 percent of the participants by act 3, and sometimes sooner. In quick starters, this growth had already reached 33 percent by the end of act 1.

Seventeen of our groups never grew to 100 percent; they fall into three distinct subtypes:

1. *Factional successes.* Nine of the groups reached a point where a majority were included in the rebellion, and only a minority signed the affidavit in act 3. Success was incomplete since the challengers were unable to convince the compliant minority to support the rebellion, perhaps because they never created any effective group pressure for resistance. Three of the nine factional successes prepared for future action. Of course, these preparations took place only among the rebellious faction rather than in the group as a whole. For some analyses, we will include these *mobilized* factional successes with other mobilized groups.

2. *Fizzlers.* Four of the groups grew to a point where a majority joined the rebellion in acts 1 and 2, yet in act 3 a majority nevertheless signed the affidavit. Indeed, in one ultra fizzler the challenger gained 100 percent support during act 2, but in the final showdown everyone signed the affidavit. The other fizzlers were at least able to hold onto a rebellious minority who refused to sign at the end.

3. *Tractables.* Four of the groups never formed a rebellious majority. In three of these, everyone signed the affidavit and in the other there was a single resister. In one ultra tractable group there was not a single act of dissent or resistance, although a fair amount of attempted evasion and rim talk occurred.

Table 5–2 summarizes the description of other rebellion careers.

REBELLION CAREER AND TYPE OF RUN

Does a successful rebellion career depend on having a planted mobilizing agent present to lead a group? Is there a connection between the type of career that an MHRC group has and the experimental variations?

Had we completed our original design, we would have been able to answer these questions with more confidence and completeness. We

TABLE 5–2   Other rebellion careers

| | | Criteria | | |
| | | Majority resistance (acts 1 and 2) | Majority resistance (act 3) | Preparation for future action |
Label	Number			
Factional successes	9	?	Yes	?
Mobilized factional successes	3	?	Yes	Yes
Fizzlers	4	Yes	No	No
Tractables	4	No	No	No

can, however, draw some conclusions from the baseline runs. It is clear enough that having a planted mobilizing agent present is far from necessary for success. Seven of the 18 baseline groups were successful, including three quick starters and four late bloomers. The other careers included six factional successes, four fizzlers, and one tractable group. Preparation for future action occurred in one-third of the baseline runs, about the same percentage as in the total sample.

Nor did our controlled variations produce any uniformity in career. The three groups in the exemplar variation divided into a quick starter, a factional success, and, surprisingly, a tractable. Even the presence of a scripted mobilizing agent failed to produce much feistiness in one of them; only one other participant joined the agent in resisting the affidavit. The three groups in the organizer variation divided into a quick starter, a late bloomer, and a factional success. As we noted earlier, however, the two successful groups produced some of the most intense and dramatic rebellion careers, including seizure of the participation agreements and especially clear and extensive preparation for future action.

In attempting to understand rebellion careers, we take note of the contribution made by our scripted mobilizing agent, and especially of his role in the two fully mobilized groups from the organizer variation. But it is quite clear that the mere presence or absence of an experimental stooge cannot account for the variations in rebellion career among the 33 groups.

SUMMARY

Rebellion career refers to the characteristic set of responses that a group makes to the dilemmas of compliance encountered during its life span. This chapter establishes the agenda for the rest of this book—to make sense of the different rebellion careers that our groups followed.

We have suggested seven types of relevant action that potential challengers may engage in when confronted with attempted regulation by authorities with whom they may not wish to cooperate: compliance, evasion, rim talk, dissent, resistance, direct action, and preparation for future action.

Among the 33 groups, we distinguished 16 successful careers marked by collective resistance to the MHRC coordinator. Seven of them were quick starters who confronted the coordinator in act 1; the other nine were late bloomers that reached the same point of collective resistance but only after a longer period of initial compliance. Nine of the successful groups prepared for future action as well, and five of these took the direct action of seizing the participation agreements.

Among the other 17 groups, nine were factional successes: a majority of the participants, while refusing to sign the affidavit, failed to achieve unanimity. Three of these factional successes also prepared for future action. The remaining eight groups had less successful rebellion careers. Four fizzlers gained a majority dissenting or resisting during acts 1 and 2, but in the act 3 showdown most or all signed the affidavit. Four tractable groups never gained a majority for the challengers, and in three of these groups everyone complied with the affidavit.

The contrasts among these careers raise questions we need to answer: What does it take for a group to manage a successful rebellion career? Why do some groups show great early promise of a successful rebellion career, only to end up as fizzlers or factional successes? In the remainder of this book, we hope to answer these questions not only for the MHRC case but for encounters with unjust authority in general.

The context of encounters 6

Every encounter has its context. It occurs at a particular place and time. People bring to it a variety of relevant attributes and attitudes that reflect the setting and influence the interaction that occurs. One can hardly hope to understand mobilization careers without some attention to this context, but precisely what should one know about it? We suggest two concepts as a useful way of talking about context: *climate* and *cleavage pattern*. Each is related to mobilization for collective action.

CLIMATE

Part of the context is historical. Presumably it makes a good deal of difference whether we're analyzing a contentious gathering in Great Britain in 1830 or in Berkeley, California, in 1964. In some times and places, there is a climate in which mobilization for collective action seems to flourish. In other periods, the climate is harsh and difficult—a winter season for would-be challengers.

Note how social movements have flourished in America under progressive national administrations. Gamson shows the 1830s, 1880s, 1890s, 1910–1920 period, and 1930s to be peak periods in the production of new challenging groups (1975: 21–22). It takes no elaborate study to add the 1960s to this time series.

It happens that with the exception of the 1880s and 1890s, these were periods in which progressive and expansive national administrations operated in Washington. In the 1830s, Andrew Jackson and his liberal successor Van Buren occupied the White House. The peak decades of the 20th century corresponded to the presidencies of Woodrow

71

Wilson, Franklin Roosevelt, John Kennedy, and Lyndon Johnson. The 1880s and 90s were exceptions—a series of conservative presidents were in office.

Progressive national administrations help to foster and maintain a political and social climate that aids the process of mobilization.[1] The idea that political climate is important in understanding this process runs through a number of discussions of protest movements. Piven and Cloward make use of it several times in analyzing poor people's movements. They discuss how the National Welfare Rights Organization and the welfare rights movement faced an increasingly unhospitable climate after 1968, the "year that the presidency passed from a liberal to a conservative leadership. With Nixon's accession to power, the class and racial injustices that had figured so prominently in the rhetoric of earlier administrations, and that had encouraged protest among the black poor, gave way to rhetoric and action emphasizing law-and-order and self-reliance, with the effect of rekindling shame and fear among the black masses. A white backlash had developed and conservative leaders acted to stimulate it all the more as a means of building support" (1975: 331–32).

Piven and Cloward make an additional point about the subtle double-edged nature of the contribution that progressive administrations make to a conducive climate for challenging groups. They suggest that this gift is a Trojan horse with a hidden cost in social control. "Early rhetorical pronouncements by liberal political leaders, including presidents of the United States, about the 'rights' of workers and the 'rights' of blacks not only helped to fuel the discontents of workers and blacks, but helped to concentrate those discontents on demands articulated by leading officials of the nation" (1977: 17).

Climate should be thought of as the product of the interaction of challenging groups and authorities. Challenging groups not only thrive in a conducive environment; through their collective action they are also important creators of the normative climate. This is easiest to see when we shift our focus to micromobilization in encounters with unjust authority. The critical episode in Fisher 1, described earlier, had a doubly favorable climate. Industrial workers were engaging in collective action all around the participants—much of it spontaneous and unplanned sit-downs. Organizing drives were underway in various major industries. At the same time, relatively sympathetic political authorities were in the saddle, and challenging group leaders were calling the recent elections a "mandate to labor to organize." Potential

---

[1] If such a conducive atmosphere somehow prevailed in the 1880s and 1890s, it must have come from somewhere other than Washington. In fact, the normative climate provided by authorities during this period was quite repressive to challenging groups. The challenges occurred for other reasons, in spite of unfavorable climate.

challengers could hardly ask for a normative climate more conducive to mobilization.

Climate of the MHRC encounter.   Fabricated though it may have been, the MHRC encounter had, like any other encounter with unjust authority, a particular historical context and climate. It occurred in a period shortly after a president of the United States had resigned from office in a far-reaching scandal that included such actions as burglaries of the files of the loyal opposition and of the professional counselors of challenging group leaders. The government's own secret police were employed to do the job on the challengers.

A decade earlier, a well-publicized incident had occurred involving General Motors, a giant corporation based in the very area in southeastern Michigan where the participants lived and worked. A critic of the corporation, concerned with the safety of the cars it was manufacturing, began collecting evidence and publicly criticizing the company. GM retaliated by hiring a private detective to investigate the private life of the critic in an effort to find material that could be used to discredit him. Not finding much usable material, the company's agents made an effort to entrap the critic in a compromising situation that could then be used for the same purpose.

The scheme didn't work. The critic fought back with a well-publicized legal suit and became a nationally known challenging group leader. The company settled out of court for a large sum of money. The critic, with a fitting sense of irony, used the money to support and sustain a continuing consumer movement.

The MHRC encounter occurred shortly after there had been much ado in the country over fuel shortages affecting driving and the heating of homes. Oil companies, much in the news, were showing large increases in profit. Gore Vidal, a well-known cynic of the day, caught the mood when he said of escapist films, popular at that time, "Such movies distract people from thoughts of robbery and deceit to which they are subjected daily by oil companies, politicians, and banks."

In our fabricated encounter, we sought to create a conducive climate for mobilization. We supposed that there was a cultural climate with which our encounter would resonate. This climate would include distrust of large oil companies, concern about invasions of privacy by companies and government, and indifference to heterosexual cohabitation by unwed adults. We expected our participants to bring this climate into the MHRC encounter and to reflect it in their response to the case of Mr. C.

What evidence do we have that this expectation was realized? We asked participants to fill out a questionnaire before presenting the case to them. Among the questions, we included pairs of statements on these issues, asking them to choose the one with which they most agreed. They were also asked to indicate the strength of their agreement with the statement closest to their feeling.[2]

There is every indication that our participants brought to the encounter a set of attitudes that reflected the anticipated climate (see Table 6–1). Fully 80 percent of them agreed that "the policies of the large oil companies usually harm the public interest," and 35 percent indicated strong agreement. Also three fourths of them agreed that "what an employee does on his own time should *not* concern his employer," and more than half of them indicate strong agreement. Almost 90 percent agreed that "the right of authorities to investigate the private lives of citizens must be severely limited," and more than two-thirds strongly agreed. Similar figures apply to the statement on associating "with an individual who is having a sexual affair."

The private beliefs of participants reflected a normative climate that was evident in their discussions of the case. It is not surprising that even heterogeneous groups found it easy to reach a consensus. There were indeed community standards in our case, and it was the oil company rather than Mr. C. who was violating them.

But perhaps our participants were unusual—not everyone answers advertisements to earn money by participating in research. They were not a probability sample of any identifiable universe, and they differed widely in their backgrounds. Perhaps we managed to recruit a group of distrustful and radical people with a chip on their shoulder about authority and big business. Perhaps our participants did not merely reflect a normative climate in their community, but were bringing in unusual predisposing attitudes that made them especially conducive to mobilization.

Our evidence suggests no special predisposition against authority or business. These participants were considerably more likely to think there was "not enough respect for authority in America nowadays" rather than too much (59 percent versus 41 percent). They are as likely to believe that "employees are treated fairly by most businesses" as that "most businesses take advantages of their employees" (52 percent versus 48 percent). There is no general climate reflected in such diverse attitudes and, not surprisingly, we find no significant relationships between mean attitudes in a group and its rebellion career.

Local climates.   It may be sunny all over Michigan but raining in Ypsilanti. Our groups were not identical in the private attitudes their

---

[2] Participants in the first six trial runs were not asked comparable questions. The data set includes the final three trial runs, the baseline runs, and systematic variations. The participants in these earliest groups were predominantly University of Michigan students, but there is no reason to expect their responses to have been more conservative than those of participants for whom we had data.

TABLE 6–1   Prior attitudes on issues directly related to the case of Mr. C.

	Agreement	Strong agreement
"The policies of the large oil companies usually harm the public interest."	80%	35%
"The policies of the large oil companies usually serve the public interest."	20%	0%
Number responding: 216		
"What an employee does on his own time should *not* concern his employer."	74%	51%
"Employers have a right to be concerned if an employee's off-the-job behavior offends the community."	26%	10%
Number responding: 216		
"Authorities should have the right to investigate the private lives of citizens."	12%	1%
"The right of authorities to investigate the private lives of citizens must be severely limited."	88%	69%
Number responding: 215		
"I wouldn't mind if I had to associate with an individual who is having a sexual affair."	90%	71%
"I would feel uncomfortable if I had to associate with an individual who is having a sexual affair."		
Number responding: 217	10%	6%

members held. Even though they may have all come from the same general climate, some may have been insulated from it for various reasons. There were, after all, 20 percent of our participants who believed that large oil companies usually serve the public interest. Suppose those 20 percent had been heavily concentrated in a few groups; the local climate in those particular groups, then, might have differed in a way systematically related to a rebellion career. In other words, having a pro-company minority bloc might have produced so much less of a conducive environment that it would have diminished the probability of such groups having a successful career. Furthermore, such a division in group opinion might well have emerged in the discussion of the case of Mr. C., presaging later internal conflict on how to respond to the dilemmas of compliance.

Local climates might make a difference in another way on questions on which there is normally considerable variance in a group. Although overall only half of the participants felt that most businesses take advantage of their employees, suppose we had had a group in which virtually everyone felt that way. Normally such an attitude is not shared by group members and does not reflect a general climate, but if everyone in a particular group happens to feel the same way it may contribute to an unusually conducive or unconducive local climate.

To explore this line of argument, we examined our groups for unusual constellations of attitudes that might have affected the group's rebellion career. By its nature, the examination could at best give hints rather than clear answers. *Unusual* in this instance means small numbers, and our numbers, none too large to begin with, were further reduced to 27 by exclusion of the early trial runs on which we had no comparable data.

Consider the following special patterns in which we might expect a local climate less conducive to a successful mobilization career:

1. Nine groups had at least a third (and two had a majority) of their members who felt that "employers have a right to be concerned if an employee's off-the-job behavior offends the community." Only one of them was successful, although four were factional successes.
2. Eight groups had at least a third of their members who felt that "the policies of the large oil companies usually serve the public interest." Only two of them were successful, but five were factional successes.
3. Six groups had two or more members from the 12 percent who believed that "authorities should have the right to investigate the private lives of citizens." Only two of them were successful, but there were three factional successes.
4. Five groups had two-thirds or more of their participants who felt that "employees are treated fairly by most businesses." Only one was successful, but there were two factional successes.
5. Participants were asked, "On most political issues, would you say you are on the liberal side, on the conservative side, or middle-of-the-road?" Only 12 percent identified themselves as conservatives. There were two groups in which there were no self-identified liberals, but two or more self-identified conservatives. Both groups were unsuccessful—a fizzler and a tractable.

Since there is substantial unreliability in such questionnaire measures, it seemed wise to demand that a group have present at least two of the above factors before being considered to have a local climate unconducive to rebellion. Figure 6–1 shows that, by this measure, climate is significantly related to success. Of the 10 groups with an unconducive climate, only 1 was successful, but nearly two-thirds of the others had a successful career. Factional successes were particularly well represented among the groups with unconducive climate; indeed, two-thirds of the nine factional successes were afflicted with this problem.

FIGURE 6–1   Climate and career

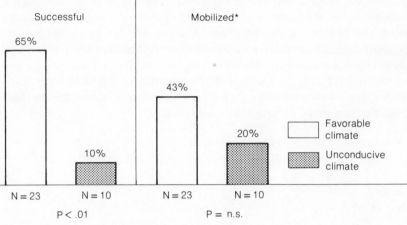

Percent

* This includes the three factional successes that prepared for future action.

The one successful group with an unconducive climate is worth noting. A majority of its members thought employers have a right to be concerned with an employee's off-the-job behavior; half of its members believed that the policies of the large oil companies usually serve the public interest; and a third of its members believed that authorities should have the right to investigate the private lives of citizens. Yet these rebellious conservatives not only achieved collective resistance, but engaged in both planning and organizing for future action against the MHRC.

We searched in vain for unusually *conducive* constellations of attitudes. A group, having already accrued the benefits of a favorable general climate, apparently gained no additional advantage by having an even more favorable local climate.

CLEAVAGE PATTERN

Every population has a set of social cleavages, a series of latent divisions or fault lines along which specific conflicts tend to flow. These cleavages are typically rooted in sustained inequalities in the population—they tend to partition people into *haves* and *have-nots* in the distribution of social rewards. On one side of the cleavage line, the population commands a disproportionate share of the society's resources.

Every encounter is embedded in a society whose social cleavages form part of its context. To understand an encounter with unjust authority, we need to understand the extent to which underlying social cleavages are being activated and made salient by it and how this may affect the process of mobilization. Assume for the moment that we establish the salience of a particular social cleavage in a given encounter. If we superimpose this cleavage on the participants in the encounter, we may partition them in a variety of different ways, each with different consequences for a rebellion career. Consider the four possible ideal types pictured in Figure 6–2.

FIGURE 6–2   Possible cleavage patterns

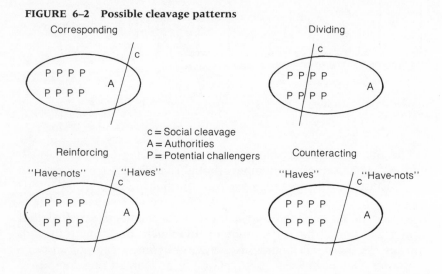

1. *Corresponding.*   In this pattern, there is no salient social cleavage that partitions the authorities from the other participants. Even if the participants have a collective identity that is related to major social cleavages, this fact will not be relevant to the encounter because it is not activated for this occasion.

2. *Reinforcing.*   In this case, a pattern of dominance and subordination present in the social context is reproduced in the encounter. The authorities are drawn from the have side of the cleavage line, and those who are being regulated are from the have-not side. The encounter in Harlem between the police and the Fruits of Islam illustrates this pattern—white authorities confronting a group of black challengers.

A reinforcing pattern has a complex effect on mobilization because it affects both the ease of mobilization and the ease of social control. On the one hand, it promotes a sense of social solidarity and collective identification. The encounter contains a "we" and a "they," and the salient cleavage operates to encourage participants to see things in these terms. Mobilization for collective action operates partly through the loyalty people feel to a group with which they identify. A reinforcing pattern helps to activate such loyalties and thereby facilitates mobilization.

On the other hand, this pattern reproduces relations of dominance and subordination that are socially sanctioned by the surrounding society. It is in the natural order of things for the haves to be exercising authority over the have-nots, and this sense of naturalness may transcend the cleavage. Potential challengers may find it natural to fall into line. Reinforcing patterns allow the interaction to run with the grain of custom, thereby facilitating social control. Reinforcing patterns, then, facilitate *both* mobilization and social control. The interplay of the encounter determines whether it is the authorities or the challengers who make greater use of the opportunities present.

3. Counteracting. In this pattern, a relationship of dominance and subordination present in the social context is reversed in the encounter. The authorities are from the have-not side of the cleavage line, and those subject to regulation are from the haves. It doesn't occur very often but, when it does, it is the pattern most facilitating to mobilization. Like a reinforcing pattern, collective identification and the operation of loyalty are stimulated. But such a pattern runs against the grain of social custom and can only complicate the task of social control by authorities.

4. Dividing. In this pattern, the salient cleavage partitions the participants into a set that includes the authority and some potential challengers and another set that includes the other potential challengers. This is bad news for mobilization. Not only is there no gain through collective identification, but the cleavage line threatens to become a basis for an internal conflict and to paralyze the ability of the group to act collectively.

Cleavage patterns in the MHRC encounter.   The MHRC scenario did not make any of the major cleavages in American society especially salient. Mr. C. is a gas station manager with a notoriously blurry social class position. Depending on what aspects of his position one wishes to emphasize, he might be variously classified. He is a small businessman and independent entrepreneur, but his work is blue-collar. We chose the position to facilitate cross-class identification. Had we made Mr. C. an automobile worker, the social class cleavage pattern would have been more relevant; we would then expect a group's pattern—whether dividing, corresponding, or reinforcing—to make a difference in its rebellion career.

Gender was not particularly salient either. In our first six trial runs, the victim in the case was a Ms. C., an assistant personnel manager who was involved in union-organizing activities. Issues of gender might well have been more salient in such a variant. An all-female group facing a male coordinator, for example, would have a reinforcing pattern with its complicated dynamics of rebellion as discussed above. But for the groups we considered in this analysis, there was nothing to make the gender cleavage particularly salient.

Nor was there anything that made race particularly salient. Mr. C.'s race is never identified. Other versions of the case could have made it more relevant. For example, we might have worked into the account that Mr. C. was black and Miss R. was white and invited the inference that racism was involved in the company's dismissal of Mr. C. Then we would expect it to make a difference whether the group confronting the white coordinator was all white, racially mixed, or all black.

Our participants also varied in age, religion, and other attributes related to social cleavages, but these evidently had even less impact than the potential cleavages mentioned above. Age, at least, is more or less publicly visible, but there was nothing in the MHRC scenario to make it relevant. Religion, in contrast, was essentially invisible to the participants; we knew it from the questionnaire, but there was no way they had of knowing such information about each other. Even if something had made a religious cleavage salient, it is hard to see how it could have affected a rebellion career.

In sum, the MHRC scenario minimized the possibility of dividing patterns by not making salient the potential cleavages that existed in our groups. Since all cleavage patterns were therefore corresponding, we expected no relationship between demographic composition of the groups and a rebellion career. And in fact, we found no correlation between the percent of women, blacks, white collar, people over 30, or any other measure of demographic composition and rebellion career.

Before we too lightly dismiss the relevance of cleavage patterns in the MHRC encounter, consider another argument. The coordinator in the encounter was in all instances a white middle-class male. Perhaps the mere happenstance that these attributes were visible made cleavage patterns relevant—even though nothing in the MHRC case emphasized them.

If such cleavages were more salient than we claim, then we need to be sensitive to differences between groups that might have put some in a dividing or reinforcing pattern instead of the assumed corresponding pattern. Our participants were mixed in occupation, but a few groups were all middle-class. Similarly with gender and race, the groups were mostly mixed, but a few had an unusual composition that might have produced an atypical cleavage pattern.

The special pattern analysis that we performed for local climates is appropriate again, this time with respect to attributes instead of attitudes. The results of such a search were negative. We explored the relevance of such special patterns as having no one over 30 in the group; having a third of the participants over 30; having two thirds or more women; having two thirds or more men; having a third or more black; having a third or more Jewish; having one third or more with no college education; and a variety of other possibilities that might conceivably produce an atypical cleavage pattern. In all cases, there was a mixture of rebellion careers found among these special patterns, with no clear preponderance of successful or unsuccessful careers. These nonrelationships provided further reason for accepting the conclusion that the MHRC encounter had a corresponding cleavage pattern that was a constant for all groups.

SUMMARY

We have argued that climate and cleavage pattern are what we want to know about the context of an encounter. In the case of the MHRC encounter, we distinguished general and local climates. The general climate was conducive to identification with the plight of Mr. C. in his battle with the oil company. But for some groups, the local climate may have been less conducive than usual. Factional successes in particular are more likely to have two or more unconducive special patterns present—thereby neutralizing some of the benefits of a favorable climate for a subsequent rebellion career. Of the 10 groups with an unconducive climate, only one was successful.

We distinguished four cleavage patterns that an encounter may have: corresponding, reinforcing, counteracting, and dividing. The MHRC encounter did not make salient any major social cleavage in American society and, hence, fits the corresponding pattern. But it is not hard to imagine variations that would make cleavages relevant, in which case we would need to pay closer attention to the cleavage pattern differences among the groups. There are good theoretical reasons for arguing that these differences would affect a rebellion career.

Assets | 7

RESOURCES

The concept of resources is an indispensable one for any discussion of power and conflict relations. Yet it remains one of the most primitive and unspecified terms in the theoretical vocabulary. Explanations abound with et cetera clauses, even among those who write most clearly and eloquently on the subject.

"Mobilization," Tilly writes, "is the process by which a group acquires collective control over the resources needed for action. Those resources may be labor power, goods, weapons, votes, and any number of other things, just so long as they are usable in acting on shared interests" (1978: 7). Dahl notes that the "base of an actor's power consists of all the *resources*—opportunities, acts, objects, etc.—that he can exploit in order to affect the behavior of another" (1957: 203). Rogers (1974) defines a resource as "any attribute, circumstance, or possession that increases the ability of its holder to influence a person or group." It appears that virtually anything can be talked of as a resource. Time, energy, hope, beauty—all enhance the ability of their holders to influence others.

The mushiness of the concept of resources becomes a particular nuisance in comparing mobilization efforts. One would like to speak of one group having more than another. But how can one make meaningful comparisons when there is (1) no agreed upon, finite set of resources to consider, (2) no unit of analysis that can be specified for many of the things designated as resources, and (3) no way of speaking of different types of resources in comparable units?

A number of writers have attempted to specify typologies of resources—a step in the right direction. Rogers, for example, distinguishes "instrumental resources" and "infra-resources." The former are the thing used to influence; "they can be used to reward, punish, or persuade. Infra-resources are those attributes, circumstances, or possessions that must be present before the appropriate instrumental resources can be activated or invoked; in that situation, they are the preconditions or prerequisites without which instrumental resources are useless" (1974: 1425).

Rogers is attempting to make some needed distinctions, but this one leaves a number of unresolved problems. It turns out that many things can be either an instrumental or infra-resource, depending on the situation. Money, for example, can be an infra-resource, and knowledge can be an instrumental resource. The problems of the et cetera clause, the lack of a specifiable unit of analysis, and the lack of comparable units for different kinds of resources remain unsolved.

Perhaps the concept of resources will prove more serviceable if we try to do less with it, using an array of concepts to do its job. Instead of making resources synonymous with anything that enhances influence or social control, we propose a much narrower usage. A *resource* must meet two additional properties:

1. Countability.   For something to be considered a resource, it must have a clearly specifiable unit. A spellbinding speaking style may be a highly useful asset in a mobilization effort. Before we consider it a resource, however, we would insist on knowing a meaningful unit of spellbindingness. Only if this requirement is met can we say unambiguously whether there is more of it in one set of potential challengers or authorities than in another.

2. Fungibility.   For something to be considered a resource, control of it must be transferable from one person or group to another. Even if we could specify a unit of spellbindingness, it wouldn't qualify as a resource unless it could be passed around. We don't mean a literal, physical transfer, but rather the passing of control. One can transfer usage rights, for example, but one can not bestow a spellbinding speaking style on another.

The votes that a head of a convention delegation controls meet such a definition of resource. The single vote is the unit and they can be promised or withdrawn. The political savvy of the delegation head, however, is not a resource nor is his photogenic profile or his charm in making a political pitch. These are useful things to have and part of his total assets, but they meet neither of our two criteria.

Analyses of large-scale mobilization processes inevitably involve comparative statements about resources, and this narrowing of the concept increases its usefulness. Tilly (1978) suggests that we focus on land, labor, capital, and technical expertise as the critical resources in the analysis of macromobilization. The first three qualify readily enough. One can specify the unit without difficulty, and each of these assets may be transferred—although fungibility of labor power may be problematic for challenging groups. Technical expertise, however, is not a resource as we have defined it, and must be considered another type of asset.

RESOURCES IN ENCOUNTERS

Resources are much less important than other assets when we shift our attention to micromobilization. To be sure, the sanctioning ability of authorities is important, and this requires resources. If they have the means of coercion to punish on the spot, this makes some kinds of collective action impossible or devastatingly costly for potential challengers.

But encounters in which challengers face large numbers of armed enforcement agents are rare. A variety of circumstances may render the social control resources of authorities irrelevant. They may, for example, be operating under constraints not to use their weapons unless attacked. In the Berkeley encounter, police could have shot the demonstrators who sat down around the police car, but they wouldn't have considered this a viable option. Hence, given the social control routines considered appropriate, their weapons are not an important resource on this occasion.[1]

A typical encounter with unjust authority involves a larger number of potential challengers facing a limited number of agents of authority. The ability of the agents to invoke future sanctions is important. In the immediate encounter, however, they cannot compel compliance and must gain it voluntarily. The authorities claim a right to regulate some aspect of the behavior of potential challengers and a corresponding obligation on the part of potential challengers to comply. The resources which they have present in the immediate encounter are largely irrelevant for this claim.

Nor are resources very important for potential challengers in such encounters. To be sure, numbers count. If only two or three people had been willing to sit down around the police car in Berkeley, they would have been quite ineffectual. They could easily enough have been removed and arrested if they had resisted. At a macro level, we consider the bodies that a social movement organization can turn out for a picket line or demonstration as a resource. This makes sense if the organization can be said to control their presence. At a micro level, the

---

[1] This is not to deny their symbolic value as a badge of authority.

presence of large numbers of potential recruits in the audience watching an encounter is not a resource, but a favorable condition or opportunity. It lacks fungibility. No individual or collective actor can deploy these numbers unless they are already organized prior to the encounter.

Hence, in the Berkeley encounter, the large numbers of spectators and passersby in Sproul Plaza made possible certain lines of collective action such as sitting down around the police car. But there were few resources of relevance in the encounter—perhaps one megaphone to address the crowd was sufficient.

KNOW-HOW

At the level of encounters, it is not resources but other assets that should draw our attention. To help identify these other assets, we examine the Berkeley encounter in more detail.

The scene was Sproul Plaza, a large open-mall area in front of the Berkeley Administration Building. Heirich (1971) describes the plaza as "home territory" for humanities and social science students, joining this leisure area of campus to a street lined with coffee shops and low-rent apartments. Sproul Plaza was a public space inhabited by students, faculty, and the many "nonstudents" in the Berkeley community—mostly one-time students at the university who continued to frequent their old haunts. They formed the potential challengers.

Although they held few resources of importance for this encounter, these potential challengers must be regarded as richly endowed for collective action. They were not organized, but many among them had a personal history containing useful political experience. The Bay Area was a major center of political activism in the early 60s. In the spring of 1960, the House Un-American Activities Committee (HUAC) held hearings in San Francisco. Public protest meetings and marches preceded the hearings, and many Berkeley people participated and provided leadership. Several hundred Berkeley students went to the opening hearing at city hall. Demonstrators who were excluded from the hearing room forced their way in and a fracas broke out. Before the affair ended, fire hoses were turned on demonstrators and some were arrested.

Many members of the Berkeley community became involved in the major civil rights demonstrations of the early 1960s. The Sheraton-Plaza Hotel in San Francisco was one major target—on grounds of employment discrimination. A series of demonstrations there resulted in more than 900 arrests, including 200 people from the Berkeley campus. Many had read about the civil rights movement, the labor movement, and other collective action efforts by challenging groups past and present. Many had talked to friends, sharing tales of past encounters. As Heirich sums it up, "Civil rights picket lines and demonstrations, antiwar demonstrations—in short, 'good causes' in the Bay Area—drew an increasing number of demonstrators" (1971: 83).

From this immersion in theory and practice, many individuals carried into Sproul Plaza important assets for collective action. How does one handle an arrest, for example? Weinberg, the man arrested in the incident, responded by "going limp." It is no coincidence that he was a member of CORE, one of the most active civil rights organizations in the Bay Area, and that this nonviolent resistance tactic was very much part of the repertoire of the civil rights movement.

Roman, the graduate student who reported shouting to others to sit down around the police car, was also a political activist—even if he had not yet become active in the emerging free speech movement. He remembered a tactic that he had learned in New York City from civil rights leader Bayard Rustin. He even had an appropriate label— *collective displacement*—to describe a procedure to be applied when demonstrators believed that the police were moving unjustly against one individual in an effort to intimidate the rest. The procedure involved the challengers confronting the police as a unit, requiring them to deal with everybody instead of one or two individuals.

Heirich also reports an account by Mike Rossman, who happened to be present in Sproul Plaza, chatting with a friend that day, and who later became a leader in the free speech movement. "I remembered San Quentin in 1960 [a demonstration against capital punishment]; we sat down around the car then—20 of us—it was probably the first car sit-around on the coast, in recent times, and I was one of them. I hadn't sat around a car for four years" (1971: 152).

Presumably it was yet another civil rights veteran who prompted the crowd into singing "We Shall Overcome" in the early moments of the sitdown—a technique designed to put a little of what Moore (1978) calls "iron in the soul." Heirich shows a dramatic photograph of a young man, Mario Savio, perched barefoot on the roof of the captured police car, addressing a crowd of several thousand spread about Sproul Plaza. It is no easy matter to hold the attention of such a large, noisy, and unruly group and deliver a speech that increases their commitment to rebellious collective action. Not everyone has the public speaking skill and presence to whip up a crowd. But Savio was already a leading spokesman for the nascent free speech movement and had polished and honed such skills in addressing earlier rallies.

The most important asset possessed by potential challengers in the Berkeley encounter was their *know-how*. Think of the craft of collective action: there are certain routines, tactics, or procedures for performing it. Know-how can be divided into *repertoire* and *skills*—that is, knowledge of collective action or social control routines and effective technique in applying them.[2]

By repertoire, we mean knowledge of how to do collective action, acquired by hearing the tales of others, reading, first-hand experience, or some combination of the above. We see evidence of knowledge of this craft in the going-limp response to the arrest, in the sit-around or collective displacement tactic, and in the singing of a movement anthem. And what we see is only the tip of the iceberg—that part of the know-how that happened to be brought into play in the particular encounter.

There is also a craft of social control, with its own procedures. Dean Murphy was clearly following such a routine when he asked Weinberg, "Are you aware that by not [removing yourself as requested] you are subjecting yourself to probable disciplinary action?" Quite obviously, Weinberg knew this, since he could see a police officer standing next to Murphy and was well aware of what was happening, but there is a routine for making an arrest that will stand up legally. Murphy's routine required that he inform Weinberg about the consequences of his rule violation. The police also had routines for dispersing a crowd; the Berkeley air was frequently filled with tear gas in the years that followed this incident, but it was not employed on this occasion.

People can apply a repertoire with varying degrees of skill. It is one thing to know that someone should address the crowd around the police car and interpret what is happening. It is another thing to be able to do this effectively. It is one thing to know that an arrest should be carried out in a manner that minimizes the provocation of bystanders, and another thing to carry out such a procedure skillfully. Skills involve the ability to use one's knowledge and resources effectively in implementing collective action or social control.

The threshold hypothesis.   Clearly we should expect a positive relationship between the richness of assets in a group of potential challengers and a successful rebellion career, but there is more than one way to specify this relationship. Take the simple linear hypothesis: the greater the assets, the higher the probability of a successful rebellion career. In this argument, with a bigger supply of resources and know-how available, challengers have a better chance of finding whatever they need to cope with situations that arise in the encounter.

The examples above suggest reasons why such a specification seems inadequate. In many encounters, there may be no great need for re-

---

[2] Tilly (1979) develops the concept of repertoire using examples from 18th and 19th century America and Britain.

sources. If one has a good megaphone to address a crowd with, what good are 20 more? Similarly, if one has a few spellbinding orators, there is nothing to be gained by having hundreds. If a significant minority has the requisite know-how and can show the way to others, not much is gained by having everybody with prior knowledge of the appropriate routines.

It is more useful to specify a desirable threshold for different kinds of assets. Those groups of potential challengers that fail to meet this threshold have a deficit with negative consequences for a rebellion career. But enough is enough. Once a group has sufficient assets, no further advantage accrues from having more.

ASSETS IN THE MHRC ENCOUNTER

The coordinator. The coordinator had no resources relevant for social control. Ordinarily, resources play their major role as the basis for constraints and inducements. But the MHRC coordinator never attempted to use sanctions against noncompliant participants and, hence, had no use for sanctioning resources. In some encounters, communication resources might be important—two-way radios, sound-amplifying equipment, and the like. No such paraphernalia was necessary for the MHRC coordinator to get his message across.

The coordinator's repertoire was constant for all groups. He had a set of established procedures for dealing with noncompliance. All of the actors playing the coordinator had the same repertoire of social control, provided by the script.

Skill is another matter. We tried to keep it constant but, in fact, it varied to some degree. In one set of three trial runs, we employed a professional actor to play the coordinator, but he made many errors in applying the designated routines. After this, we relied on two principal coordinators. Both applied the routines with very few errors, but there were subtle differences between them. To the extent that we became aware of differences, we attempted to eliminate them as much as possible.

Both principal coordinators improved their skill with practice.[3] For example, we became aware that the coordinator sometimes seemed to be inviting questions by lingering too long after giving instructions. Both coordinators began to exit more promptly in later runs, but there were still some slight differences between their exit speeds. Despite such differences, there was no overall relationship between the person playing the coordinator and a rebellion career.

---

[3] The skill of the coordinator, we should note, was not aimed at achieving the most effective social control possible but in carrying out a particular social control routine as

Both principal coordinators produced about the same proportion of successful and unsuccessful groups. Each handled nine of the baseline runs, which provide the most meaningful comparison. In these, one coordinator presided over two quick starters, a late bloomer, three factional successes, and three fizzlers; the other presided over a quick starter, three late bloomers, three factional successes, a fizzler, and a tractable. While differences in skill undoubtedly existed, they did not appear to be systematic enough or substantial enough to cause a problem. Nonetheless, we will remain attentive to possible differences in coordinator style when we examine the interaction in the encounter.

The potential challengers.   Few, if any, resources were needed to take action against the MHRC. Participants sometimes planned meetings, but they were a small enough group that they could easily find public space to get together. They planned phone calls and, indeed, we did have an instance in which one participant offered a dime to one who had suggested a plan to call the Better Business Bureau about what the MHRC was doing. There was no scarcity of this resource at the level of need in an MHRC encounter. Participants sometimes exchanged names and addresses, but this presented no resource problems since pencils and paper were provided. The collective action possibilities present in the MHRC encounter didn't require any significant resources.

Potential challengers do need know-how. The skills involved are basically group process and communication skills—how to get people's attention, how to move a group toward a decision, and the like. Not every MHRC group was equally endowed with persons possessing such skills, however. The coordinator, for example, parried the questions put to him and attempted to evade them with the claim that he was only following instructions. Some participants had learned a bag of tricks for dealing with such bureaucratic dodges. The tactic of whistle-blowing—that is, exposing the MHRC with unfavorable publicity—was in some repertoires, and lacking in others. We expected differences among our groups in how richly endowed they were with potential challengers with know-how.

Measurement strategy.   The distinction between skills and repertoire is an analytic one. In practice, they are typically merged in the same activity. If we ask, for example, whether dealing with the mass media involves skill or knowledge of routines, the answer is both.

---

faithfully as possible. The most difficult task that the coordinator faced was to present the demands of the MHRC clearly and firmly in the face of sometimes impassioned attempts of participants to negotiate a reasonable compromise.

Knowing whom to contact with a press release or statement is part of one's repertoire; making the statement in a persuasive fashion is a skill.

Rather than attempting to measure such assets directly, we look at the experiences that tend to produce know-how. In particular, we look at the prior educational, organizational, and political experiences of the participants. By inferring know-how from such experiences, we avoid a serious problem of tautology. One might be tempted to measure skill, for example, by watching who manifests it in an encounter. But this blurs the concept of assets by destroying the distinction between the potential in a group and what is actually accomplished. Unless we have an independent prior measure of potential, we cannot hope to make statements about the degree to which different groups realize their potential. Some groups are well-endowed but do not make effective use of their assets; others get more mileage out of smaller endowments. By inferring assets from measures that are independent of what happens, we avoid such problems of tautology.

On the questionnaire administered at the beginning, participants were asked their highest level of education and their experience with a variety of voluntary associations. We were reluctant to ask them about their political experiences at this point for fear of generating suspicion of the fabrication. Hence we asked a number of questions on such matters only during the debriefing period, when participants knew of the hoax and its general purposes. Given the nature of the research, we must be wary of some exaggeration in the extent of such reported political participation.

Such a bias, if it exists, is a constant one for all groups and should not affect the validity of relative differences in reported political activity. In the postquestionnaire, participants were asked if they had ever participated in a protest demonstration, attended political meetings or rallies, participated in a wildcat strike, participated in a union-authorized strike, worked for a political candidate, challenged the order of a policeman, teacher, or employer, or engaged in any other activity where they challenged someone's authority. They were also asked to indicate the degree of activity for each category checked. From such questions on education, voluntary association activity, and political activity, we hoped to assess the relative know-how of the MHRC groups.[4]

Deficits. Most of our groups turned out to be naturally endowed with participants who had had a fair amount of organizational and political experience. In addition, three of them were given an

---

[4] Again we lack comparable data on the first six trial runs, and these are excluded from the analysis that follows. Since five of these six trial runs included a planted mobilizing agent who brought additional know-how to the group in an unmeasured way, the exclusion of these groups also simplifies interpretation.

"organizer"—a scripted mobilizing agent who had at hand a set of routines to introduce at appropriate moments. Furthermore, our organizers were played by individuals with a background of political activism that had provided them with opportunitities to acquire and hone relevant skills.

Some groups, however, appeared to be lacking in the usual know-how. Four such deficits:

1. Deficit in organizational activists. Participants indicated whether they belonged to different voluntary associations and circled the names of those in which they had been "very active." Most groups had *at least* two people who claimed to be very active in some voluntary association, but there were seven groups with less than two such organizational activists in their ranks. Only one of the seven was successful, and it turned out to be an ultra-late bloomer, a group that was tractable through acts 1 and 2. The remaining six included three fizzlers and two tractables.

2. Deficit in college-educated. Six groups had either a majority of participants with no college education or no one who was a college graduate. None of these groups were successful and only one managed even a factional success.

3. Deficit in political demonstrators. Participants were asked to indicate how frequently they had participated in "protest demonstrations." Most of them claimed to have done so, something which we are disinclined to take at face value. The vagueness of the term and the posthoax context would appear to encourage over-reporting of such participation. If we use a higher cut-off point for reported activity, we find four groups with no one who claims to have participated in two or more demonstrations. None were successful and three of the four were fizzlers.

4. Deficit in strikers. Every group save one had participants who claim to have participated in a strike. The one exception was unsuccessful.

As Figure 7–1 indicates, there were 11 groups that had at least one of the above deficits. Only one (an ultra-late bloomer) was successful, but it failed to mobilize. In contrast, almost two-thirds of the groups with adequate know-how were successful and more than half mobilized. Every fizzler and tractable had at least one deficit and three of the four fizzlers had more than one. Lack of adequate know-how did appear to be handicapping a significant number of groups in their subsequent rebellion career.

Surpluses. We argued earlier that beyond a necessary threshold, no advantage was gained by adding further assets. Our evidence tends to support this argument. We examined a number of special patterns that might be expected to produce especially well-endowed groups. We

FIGURE 7–1   Know-how and rebellion career

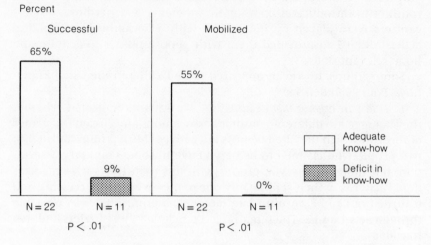

included the presence of an unusual number of people who reported especially high participation in protest demonstrations, in strikes, in voluntary association activity, and in organizing demonstrations or meetings. Groups with extra assets were not significantly more successful than the others. Of 16 successful groups, only 9 had at least one such surplus, while 7 of the 9 factional successes had surplus know-how.

The three groups to which we added an organizer were all naturally well endowed with know-how and had no deficits. Indeed, one of the three groups in the organizer variation had the richest natural assets of any group in the sample. In adding an organizer, we may have been merely gilding the lily.

Group size.   The MHRC groups ranged in size from 6 to 10 participants—a restricted range but perhaps enough to make a difference. One increases many things with size. On the one hand, more potential carriers of know-how might lead one to expect a positive relationship between size and rebellion career. On the other hand, size increases complexity of coordination. A group of 10, for example, has three times as many dyads and six times as many triads as a group of six. It would seem that much harder to gain collective resistance among 10 people than among 6.

It turned out there was very little relationship between size and rebellion career among our 33 groups. The 16 successful groups averaged 7.8 members against 7.5 for the unsuccessful groups, an insignificant difference. Nor did size predict preparation for future action.

The 12 groups in which such activity occurred averaged 7.67, exactly the same as the other 21. Variation in group size is something we can safely ignore in the MHRC encounter.

SUMMARY

In the past two chapters, we considered how differences in what the participants brought into the encounter could account for differences in their rebellion careers. In the previous chapter, we considered the participants' attitudes and attributes for what they tell us about climate and cleavage patterns in the MHRC encounter.

In this chapter, we focused on the know-how reflected in the prior organizational and political experiences of the potential challengers. We argued that the assets of the coordinator were held more or less constant. For the potential challengers, resources were not important, but other assets such as repertoire and skills did affect rebellion career. In particular, certain groups suffered from one or more deficits in know-how—and the ones that did, did not happen to have our scripted organizer to bail them out. The tractables and fizzlers in particular seemed to suffer from such deficits. Surplus know-how, which did not seem to add much to a rebellion career, was particularly likely to be present among factional successes.

We have not fully exhausted the relevance of what people brought to the encounter. In subsequent chapters, we will turn our attention again to the ensuing interaction as we try to unpack the process of micromobilization. In doing so, we will consider the significance of a number of acts that further the rebellion career of a group; we will examine, among other issues, the prior attitudes, attributes, and experiences of the individuals who are most likely to perform them.

Working together | 8

When a challenging group takes on some set of authorities, there is a fundamental asymmetry between the actors engaged in the conflict. Authorities are typically organized in a hierarchy with agents at their command who are likely to be paid employees, functioning in well-defined organizational roles.

For challengers, organization is inherently more problematic and less to be taken for granted. A challenger may have no willing agents but only sympathizers, some fervent and others easily distracted. As a collective entity, it is typically something in the process of becoming, not an accomplished fact. The nascent quality of its organization is especially apparent at the level of encounters. It is bravado when Bud Simons tells the Fisher 1 plant manager, "It's the union you're talking to right now, Mr. Parker." The union is still only a hope emerging, with the encounter as midwife for the nascent challenging group.

We don't wish to overdraw this contrast between the organizational problems of challengers and authorities. The operatives of authorities are not always willing to behave like good agents. Mutinies and defections of soldiers in revolutionary situations provide striking examples of such problematic encounters for authorities. Here, even the loyalties of officers and their willingness to perform in role cannot be taken for granted. Defection of agents to the challenger can be a serious problem for authorities in a variety of encounters and might well be considered an important index of success for a challenger.

Nor are challenging groups always without agents. Indeed, they are engaged in the process of creating voluntary agents, drawing them from their constituency. The union had the beginnings of a cadre in

Fisher 1—a set of members who had been instructed on "how to act in case of surprise developments." To be sure, the roles of these "volunteer organizers" were not very well defined compared to such roles as foreman and plant manager. But agency is a matter of degree and the union already had taken a step in this direction.[1]

We are concerned in this chapter with the development of challenging groups as nascent organizations and with the acts that further their organizational development. The bulk of such development takes place in meetings or informal interactions among members and sympathizers, away from the public arena of confrontations with authorities. Encounters with unjust authority, however, are frequently proving grounds, testing the degree to which various organizational problems have been solved.

ORGANIZATIONAL DEVELOPMENT OF THE CHALLENGER

Tests are also opportunities, in this case, opportunities to further the capacity for acting together. Our analysis focuses on organizing acts—that is, any word or deed by a challenger that furthers the ability of participants to act as a group. More specifically, these acts further one of three central organizational processes.

Building loyalty to the challenger.   Challengers are engaged in a contest with authorities for the allegiance of uncommitted constituents. These constituents may be angry at the authorities and ready to take action against them without feeling any solidarity with other participants or allegiance to the challenging group sponsoring the action. Some of the workers in Fisher 1 who supported the sit-down may have been unsympathetic or even hostile to the union, but mad enough at the company to go along.

The long-run organizational goal is to build loyalty to the challenging group per se so that it is treated by the constituency as something worth fostering and defending against attack. Loyalty-building proceeds in stages: from identification with a solitary group to commitment to a specific organization. Solidarity is rooted in the relationships linking the members of a group to one another. People may be linked together in a number of ways that generate a sense of common iden-

---

[1] Sometimes challengers have third party agents, persons from allied groups who are attempting to foster their mobilization for collective action. These agents usually are overt, with potential challengers aware that they have been lent by a fraternal ally as resources for the challenging group. There are numerous examples of more established unions assigning paid organizers to aid another fledgling union in the mobilization of its separate constituency.

tity, shared fate, and general commitment to defend the group. Words or deeds in an encounter may underline the common fate or shared outlook of participants, or demonstrate their willingness to make sacrifices on behalf of the group.

In the Berkeley encounter, Weinberg demonstrated that he was willing to be arrested defending the general right of members of the Berkeley community to engage in political activity on campus. The act was intended and perceived as defense of a collective interest, not a personal one. The basis for solidarity was a shared principle or moral code, and Weinberg's action asserted an implicit claim of solidarity with a constituency of Berkeley political activists.

Loyalty-building acts may go beyond enhancing group solidarity, to promoting allegiance to a specific challenging organization. This more advanced stage of loyalty-building was largely absent in the Berkeley encounter since an organizational carrier for the free speech movement had not yet emerged. In the Flint encounter, however, the UAW existed and was attempting to establish itself as an effective instrument for pursuing the principles and interests of automobile workers.

Allegiance is something that a challenger must earn. One important way it earns it is by having individuals who are identified with the organization take personal risks on behalf of the challenging group. In the Fisher 1 encounter, Simons and his allies were known as union men. They were prepared to risk their jobs in the midst of the depression, acting in the name of the union. These risks on behalf of other workers affirmed the union as an organization worthy of important personal sacrifices.

Simons was also engaged in loyalty-building when he presented himself as a spokesman for the union, telling the plant manager, "Now we've organized ourselves into a union. It's the union you're talking to right now, Mr. Parker." He did this when he spoke in the name of the constituency: "That's what the men say. . . . Nobody is going to work until [the Perkins brothers are back on the job]." His claim was later backed up by a successful strike vote.

The most important contribution to loyalty-building in this and many other encounters stemmed from the outcome. Kraus (1947) tells how the return of the Perkins brothers to work produced a "deafening cheer that could be heard in the most distant reaches of the . . . plant." A great deal of loyalty-building can easily go to naught without a bit of success for a booster.

Managing the logistics of collective action. Compared to long-term mobilization efforts, the logistics required for collective action in encounters are relatively minor. Still, a variety of matters may arise requiring some operating procedures. With a relatively established challenger that has some infrastructure and assigned roles, this may be no great problem. But the mechanics of acting together can present some serious problems for less organized challengers.

In the Fisher 1 encounter, the union could not completely control the composition of the negotiating committee. Because of this failure, the challengers were especially vulnerable to attempts by authorities to ignore the union and deal with the workers as individuals. "Now I didn't ask you," the plant manager would say. "You can talk when it's your turn" (Kraus, 1947: 53).

The challengers were also called upon to manage the logistics of a critical strike vote. Simons, on behalf of the challengers, initiated what amounted to a vote of confidence or no-confidence in the union. A defeat in such a vote would have been a devastating set-back for the challenger, but Simons was no doubt confident that the union could control the meeting and strengthen its hand with a ringing endorsement of its position. Part of his confidence came from knowing that he could count on a sizable cadre of union activists to look out for the interests of the challenger during the critical meeting preceding the vote.

Apparatus building provides procedures for carrying out collective action. In Fisher 1, some of the necessary apparatus building had been done beforehand. The UAW organizer assigned to Flint had instructed the union cadre on how to come together at a given spot in the plant, reach quick decisions, and take appropriate steps. The challengers had people who knew how to run a strike vote. Encounters with unjust authority are occasions to utilize an apparatus rather than construct it, but improvisation may frequently be called for in spite of the most careful preparation.

Managing internal conflict. Some kinds of internal disagreement in an organization may increase its effectiveness by subjecting its strategy and program to valid criticism, thereby generating improvements. But an encounter with unjust authority is not the time for a challenger to work through its internal disagreements and factional disputes. Given the adversarial nature of the encounter, such public disagreement makes the challenger vulnerable to divide-and-conquer tactics by authorities and diminishes the potential for collective action. Challengers need to avoid a situation in which internal disagreements lead to two or more separate and conflicting lines of action.

Plenty of internal conflict existed in the UAW but it was successfully prevented from emerging in the encounter. The original UAW organizer in Flint had been recalled a few months earlier in a bit of political infighting. Bitter internal battles ensued in later years between left-wing and more moderate factions. But during the Fisher 1 encounter and the great sit-down strike that was to occur six weeks later, such conflicts were muted and no single faction could claim a monopoly of heroes. Fine describes the prevailing view at that time by quoting a rubber worker who was aiding the UAW organizing effort. "It doesn't make any difference if a man is a Communist, Socialist, Republican, or Democrat, as long as he is loyal to the union" (1969: 93).

Conflict managing makes it less likely that internal disagreements will produce separate and conflicting lines of action in the encounter. There are two paths to this end. First, one can contest and discredit a competing line of action or its advocates, leaving it without any significant support. Showing advocates of a competing line of action to be *agents provocateur* or company spies serves such a purpose. Alternatively, the challenger may find common ground between disagreeing parties and seek a modus vivendi that will prevent a split during the encounter.

Kraus does not give us much detail on how disagreements were handled in the encounter in Fisher 1. Given the presence of company sympathizers among the workers and their varying degrees of militancy and commitment to the union, it is safe to assume that disagreements arose. Apparently such disagreements were handled successfully, for we have no evidence of any attempt at a separate and conflicting line of action by a faction.

In sum, organizing is accomplished through a series of specific words or deeds that build loyalty, manage internal conflict, and provide solutions to logistical problems. Much of this organizing work takes place in internal meetings when authorities are not present. Encounters with unjust authority provide opportunities to carry such processes forward and thereby increase the ability of challengers to act in a coordinated way.

It takes time for a challenger to get sufficiently organized for collective action. During the course of this process, the degree of loyalty that any given person gives to the challenger may fluctuate. Furthermore, different individuals in an encounter may vary widely in their loyalty to the challenger at any given moment. New situations may call for ingenuity in devising appropriate procedures for collective action. Internal disagreements may wax or wane. The MHRC encounter, beginning as it did with unorganized strangers, compressed these organizational processes into the course of a single encounter. We now turn to it to examine organizing in operation.

ORGANIZING ACTS IN THE MHRC ENCOUNTER

Even in an encounter as brief as the MHRC scenario, it is possible for a challenging group to gain loyalty. This frequently became manifest in act 3 when the coordinator presented the affidavit. Some participants who refused to give false opinions told the coordinator, "I didn't personally say anything I didn't believe, but I'm not going to sign this either, if the rest of the group isn't signing." Many were uncertain at this point, waiting to see what others would do, delaying decision as long as possible. Ultimately, they were faced with an unavoidable choice—to sign or not to sign—and loyalty to the group became one major factor in their decision.

Loyalty building.   Loyalty building in the MHRC situation focused on creating a sense of collective identity among participants. There were three specific acts that seem promising for such a purpose:

1. Consensus calling.   Participants sometimes say things that make a group aware of its shared outlook. When they call attention to the consensus, they are underlining a basis for solidarity—in this case, a common set of moral standards. One might expect this act to further a rebellion career.

The first open discussion of the case of Mr. C. provided the perfect opportunity for this consensus calling to occur. Groups reached consensus in varying degrees. Some found a lowest common denominator while others discovered they were like-minded on a broader range of issues. The relatively low consensus groups could agree that, whatever you think of Mr. C.'s behavior, it didn't constitute sufficient grounds for firing him. This consensus papered over the fact that they differed to some degree about what constitutes a proper lifestyle.

In other groups, the consensus was deeper than this. Mr. C.'s lifestyle didn't offend their standards, but the way the oil company acted did. Even in groups where this stronger consensus develops, it may remain tacit and unacknowledged. But in one-third of the MHRC groups, there was explicit consensus calling at this point. The transcript below illustrates the process:

Margie: Would anyone here really object to their next door neighbor living with somebody else unmarried? That, that's the big question. I don't think anybody here does.

Tim: No.

Barbara: No.

Margie: So that really is the morals of the community right here. [*pausing for group laughter*] Is there anything else that has to be said? [*group laughter*]

Frank: I think we've summed up our morals, come to a poll.

As Figure 8–1 shows, there is very weak support for the hypothesis that consensus calling is important in a group's rebellion career. Groups in which it occurred were not significantly more successful, it never occurred in a majority of the successful groups, and it occurred in half of the fizzlers. Perhaps the issues in the case of Mr. C. seemed so

FIGURE 8-1   Consensus calling and career

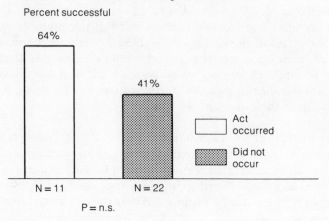

Percent successful

blatant to many people that the mere discovery that everyone agreed didn't provide much of a boost for group solidarity.

2. Protest humor.   Roy (1978) argues that irony is a manifestation of in-group solidarity and out-group hostility. It functions, she suggests, to separate the groups into "us" versus those "outsiders" against whom we have hostile feelings. She experimentally manipulated in-group cohesion and out-group hostility (the latter via frustration with the experimenter) and found differential use of irony in support of the above argument. We followed her logic but reversed the flow of causality. Protest humor was viewed as a means by which a group created its own in-group solidarity in opposition to the coordinator.

The coding of irony is very complex and time-consuming. Roy relied upon intonational cues such as nasalization and exaggerated stress on one or more parts, as well as on contextual cues that are difficult to systematize. We relied on a simpler, more reliable measure, based on laughter as a response to certain utterances. Since the coordinator never attempted to joke with the group, laughter at his instructions or his defense of MHRC procedures was always *derisive* laughter. We coded this whenever it occurred.

Sometimes participants made remarks about MHRC procedures that drew laughter. From content alone, there was no reliable way of inferring humorous intent, but by using the response of laughter we avoided having to make such inferences. Presumably, something in the timing, context, or tone of voice was picked up by other participants and this was sufficient for our purposes. Some examples of such protest humor:

Coordinator: These procedures were designed by fully competent people who know what they're doing.
[*The group laughs derisively.*]

Travis: Did you see the movie, *Kurlack's View?* This really seriously has a bearing on this. [*group laughter*] In it, an ad was placed in the paper for help wanted, and what it turned out to be was trained killers. A very innocuous beginning and they wound up as trained killers. [*group laughter*]

[*The same group in a later scene*]

Linda: Excuse me. I'm a little bit put off by this. [*group laughter*] We are very moral people.

Travis: Right, and we have $10 in our pocket. [*group laughter*] And we don't want to be faced with the situation where you read in the *New York Times* one day that thanks to a new method in litigation [*group laughter*] that this poor schnook [*group laughter*] has lost his license.

Coordinator: Well, you don't have to worry . . .

Travis: Well, that's what Nixon said. [*group laughter*]

[*A different group*]

Coordinator: . . . so we'd like you to take the position of someone who's offended by Mr. C.'s behavior.

Carol: But that would be so hard 'cause I really—that is something that I so strongly wouldn't, I couldn't even have a defense.

Coordinator: I don't think you'll find it that difficult.

Carol: Oh, don't do it to me! [*laughter; then as Coordinator exits:*] But wait a second on it. Don't have me do that. [*group laughter*] Maybe someone older. [*group laughter*]

Protest humor—where the group was, in effect, making fun of the coordinator and the MHRC—occurred by the end of act 2 in about 80 percent of the groups, and it occurred in the opening scene in more than a third. We have argued that it would enhance a rebellion career by promoting group solidarity, and our data provide only weak support for this hypothesis. As Figure 8–2 shows, two thirds of the groups where it occurred in the opening scene went on to a successful rebellion career. The successful percentage declines to less than one third for those groups in which protest humor was not employed before act 3. However, the numbers are small here, and differences of this magnitude are not statistically significant.

3. *Speaking for the group.* A participant can promote a collective orientation most strongly and directly by adopting the role of spokesperson. Operationally, we look for statements in which a participant declares a belief, opinion, or intended action to be held *by the group*.[2] To do this is to present an implicit claim that the aggregate of individuals form a unit.

---

[2] We do *not* include here statements in which the group is merely the object of a declaration of belief or intent—for example, "It's wrong to ask us to give false opinions," or "We were asked to give our opinions but not to give false opinions."

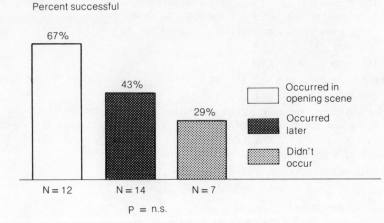

FIGURE 8–2   Protest humor and career

Percent successful

Adopting this role can be risky. There is always the danger that someone will say, "Speak for yourself." But each unchallenged repetition embeds the collective orientation more deeply. Most important of all, others may adopt the role as well, creating multiple spokespersons in a group. The existence of several persons speaking for the group both reflects the development of a collective orientation and reinforces it with each repetition until it is taken for granted.

The transcripts below provide examples of speaking for the group:

Coordinator: Apparently you didn't understand. It's necessary for you to talk as if you actually are a member of the community who's offended . . .

Betsy: I think *you* didn't understand it. We do understand it and we don't want to go on record, even pretending that we agree with what we're saying. We don't. All three of us feel the same way. I think everyone of us feels that way here.

[*A different group*]

Jenny: [*addressing the camera just after the coordinator has exited*] OK. We were just asked, for the sake of the camera and to get a balanced view, to lie. Three members of our group were said to go against what they feel for the sake of public discussion. And when we came in here tonight, we were told to tell the truth because we are a representative sample. And we are being asked to go against our integrity for $10 apiece.

[*A different group*]

Betty: How are people going to know that these aren't our opinions?

Coordinator: I don't think you need to worry about that. We'll take care of it.

Bob: I think we do need to worry about it.

Does it enhance the rebellion career of a group to have various people speaking for it? Just having one person do it is not enough.

There is no significant relationship between the mere presence of a spokesperson and success, as all of the fizzlers and a majority of the factional successes had someone speaking for the group. It is only when the collective orientation is reflected by more than one person that a clear relationship to success emerges.

As Figure 8–3 shows, more than 80 percent of the groups with multiple spokespersons had successful careers, while less than one third of the others managed this feat. One of the exceptions was the ultra-fizzler described earlier—a group that had everyone protesting at one point but everyone signing the affidavit in the end. This group had all of our loyalty building acts: consensus calling, lots of protest humor, and multiple spokespersons. There was no evidence that they lacked solidarity, and indeed, their response was collectively compliant in the end. Other processes—particularly reframing—were not handled as well, perhaps reflecting their triple deficit in know-how.

FIGURE 8–3   Multiple spokespersons and career

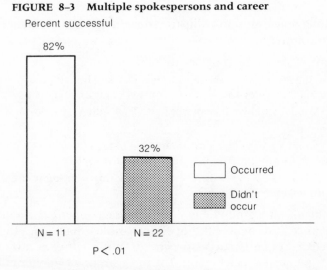

Percent successful

82%

32%

☐ Occurred

▨ Didn't occur

N = 11   N = 22

P < .01

Conflict managing.   Conflict managing in the MHRC encounter centered on preventing the emergence of a loyalist faction that would eventually support the coordinator in act 3 by signing the affidavit. Disagreement occurred earlier, before the affidavit, on how to handle dilemmas of compliance. About 80 percent of our groups had some form of disagreement on such issues before act 3, and the same percentage had someone who advocated compliance, i.e., giving false opinions. Only three groups had neither disagreement nor compliance advocacy. Hence, some conflict over compliance or protest strategy is almost always a problem that a group must face.

We measured two kinds of conflict managing in the MHRC encounter.

1. Patching disagreements. Here we look at the extent to which disagreements that arise are followed by agreement among contending parties, or are left unresolved. There are different paths to agreement. In some cases, a third party makes a statement to which two previously disagreeing parties concur. The third party has found some common ground between the contestants. In other cases, the contesting parties find some common ground between themselves. This happens when one party disagrees with another, and then either one says something else that produces agreement.

2. Countering compliance advocacy. This form of conflict managing might be called *nipping-in-the-bud.* Sometimes when participants advocate compliance with instructions to give false opinions, they get no disagreement from others. In other scenes, or in other groups, advocacy of compliance draws explicit disagreement or counteradvocacy in response.

The following transcript illustrates compliance advocacy and attempts to counter it:

Bernice: Well, I'd say they can take back the money.

Gertrude: If he wants his 10 bucks, I'll give it back to him, for the love of God! [*pause*] I'll play devil's advocate because I enjoy an argument, ah . . .

Bernice: Just do it and we'll be out of here. That's the way I look at it.

Gertrude: No.

Harold: I wonder what's going to, ah, happen to the guy. [*pause*] If it's around here where you can, uh, when they have the trial . . .

Bernice: I don't see why—how they could use this, you know. Because we aren't celebrities or anything.

It is difficult for a group to avoid some disagreement over dilemmas of compliance and, hence, the need for conflict managing. Disagreement occurred often in successful groups, but it either occurred early or, if late, got quickly patched up. The most striking evidence of failure to develop a collective orientation was the presence of unresolved disagreements during the final two scenes before the affidavit. As Figure 8–4 shows, there were 13 groups with late, unresolved disagreements, and only one of them was successful. In contrast, 75 percent of those groups that avoided such late disagreements were successful.

The postfabrication questionnaire offers some additional supporting evidence on conflict managing and success. Participants were asked how much they were bothered by various things that occurred during the course of the scenario, including whether they were bothered "by the way some people cooperated with the coordinator." There were eight groups in which a third or more indicated that they were

FIGURE 8–4   Unresolved disagreements and career

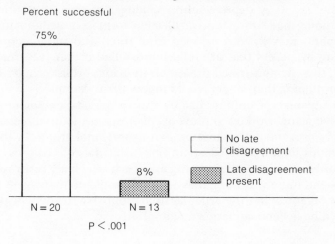

Percent successful

75%

8%

No late
disagreement

Late disagreement
present

N = 20   N = 13

P < .001

bothered by such compliance; only one of them was successful. This seemed to be a particular issue among the factional successes; five of the nine showed this level of retrospective disagreement, including all three of the mobilized factional successes.

Again, the deviant case is of interest—the one group that succeeded in spite of considerable evidence of internal conflict. This group had unresolved disagreements in four separate scenes, more than any of the other 32 groups. It was also the only successful group meeting our criterion of disagreement on the postfabrication questionnaire. It turns out that this exceptional case was the final MHRC encounter, one of the two groups that led to our halting the fabrication. Watching the tape, one is struck by the heterogeneity of this group in education and social class. Our questionnaire data bear out this impression, revealing an education range from less than ninth grade to graduate study.

This group contained a planted organizer, who played some role in the extended sequence of disagreements. Our coding reveals that this mobilizing agent did two things that rather rarely occur spontaneously. First, he repeatedly challenged compliance advocacy, a recurrent problem in the group. On three separate occasions he disagreed with participants who advocated going along with giving false opinions. He also attempted to dissuade a participant who indicated an intention to walk out during act 2, urging him to stay with the group and see the situation through.

Walk-outs before act 3 occurred in only three groups—two factional successes and a fizzler. These walk-outs were disruptive events for a group, depriving it of its participants most likely to lead a rebellion. To use Hirschman's (1970) terms, by choosing exit instead of voice as a strategy, they deprived the challenger of the contribution they might have made to a more collective form of rebellion. Impatient participants may have concluded from internal disagreement or foot dragging by others that any effective unified action was impossible. Hence, they demonstrated their own individual resistance by leaving, perhaps hoping that others would follow their example.

Our organizer, committed as he was to the challenging group as a collective actor, worked to prevent this response to disagreement and probably prevented a premature exit in this final group. In the other two groups with a scripted organizer, his actual role was less critical, since only one disagreement arose in each—in both cases relatively early—and there was not much internal conflict to manage. But without the organizer in this particular final group, we strongly suspect that it would have been, at best, a factional success.

Apparatus building. Apparatus building in the MHRC encounter was used as an outcome measure, our benchmark for whether a group prepared for future action. The measures have been discussed and illustrated earlier, specifically, whether a group discussed plans for whistle-blowing and whether they took steps to meet afterward.

WHO WERE THE SPOKESPERSONS?

Organizing acts are performed by individuals. Since we have argued that these acts require know-how, we might suspect that the more highly educated people with organizational and political experience are the ones helping the group develop its collective orientation.

There were 42 individuals who spoke for a group before act 3, two of them planted mobilizing agents (eliminated from the subsequent analysis). We have a substantial amount of questionnaire data on most of them, and it is instructive to ask in what ways they differed from their fellow participants.[3]

With one exception over a wide range of characteristics, there was no significant difference. Their average education, for example, was no higher than the rest, although there was a slight underrepresentation at both the high and low end. The model spokesperson had some college but was not a college graduate.

There was one surprise: 80 percent of the spokespersons were women! We expected that men would be overrepresented, but in fact there was a significant difference in the opposite direction.

---

[3] Ten spokespersons were in early trial runs for which we lack questionnaire data, reducing the number to 30 for most of our comparisons.

SUMMARY

For a successful rebellion career, participants must ultimately adopt a shared response. It is difficult to achieve this among a group of heterogeneous strangers. Somehow, participants must come to see their fellow group members as comrades—even if only for a brief occasion.

By engaging in a series of organizing acts during the first part of the scenario, the MHRC participants were able to increase their capacity for working together at the end. These organizing acts enhanced loyalty to the challenger, created some procedure or apparatus for managing logistical problems, or handled internal conflicts so they didn't disrupt collective action.

Almost all apparatus building in the MHRC encounter occurred after the affidavit had been introduced. Hence it was used here as a measure of success rather than as an explanation of it. We focused on loyalty building and conflict managing in the first two acts. With respect to loyalty building, there was weak support for the hypotheses that consensus calling and protest humor are related to success. The most important loyalty-building act, however, was speaking for the group and, in particular, the development of multiple spokespersons. Almost all groups that achieved this organizing benchmark eventually succeeded.

Conflict managing also had a clear relationship to a successful career. Internal disagreements over handling the dilemmas of compliance occurred to some degree in almost all groups, but in many it was resolved early and didn't recur in the late scenes of act 2. Only one group with such late, unresolved disagreement succeeded and, our evidence suggests, it was helped substantially by skillful efforts of our planted mobilizing agent who played an active role in conflict managing.

The more a group learns to act together, the easier time it will have with other processes. It is a great deal easier for potential challengers to repudiate an obligation to comply when they speak with a sense of group support. It is a great deal easier to arrive at a shared interpretation of what is happening when they already share a sense of solidarity. Working together is important, but it is only one part of the process.

Breaking out | 9

Rebellion is an extraordinary event. When a boss tells us to start working, most of us start working. When a cop tells us to move along, most of the time we move along. When an usher tells us to form a line, most of us queue up. We spend a large portion of our lives compliantly acting out roles in authority systems of one sort or another, accepting daily regulation as a matter of course.

Compliance with authority is so common that some consider it a habit or a conditioned response. Kraus (1947), in his description of the Fisher 1 encounter, uses such language to describe the tension some workers felt as the assembly line started up and they stood in place without working. "Habit was deep in them, and it was like physical agony for them to see the bodies pass untouched. They grabbed their tools and chased after them." But "habit" is merely a label, not an explanation. To demystify the forces that bond us in authority systems, we need to look deeper into the reasons for compliance.

SELF-INTEREST

Authorities typically have an array of inducements and constraints available to aid them in social control.[1] In some encounters, defiance can mean arrest, beatings, and even execution. Those who refuse to accept regulation may lose their job or suffer personally in other important ways. On the inducement side, those who go along, get along.

---

[1] We use these terms as in Gamson (1968: 75–77): "Constraints are the addition of new disadvantages to the situation or the threat to do so. . . . Inducements are the addition of new advantages to the situation or the promise to do so."

A demonstration of a willingness to accept regulation can lead to future rewards of various sorts. The benefit of the doubt goes to those who cooperate.

Of course, one's self-interest depends on what one is being asked to do. A soldier, ordered to carry out a particularly dangerous mission, may find his interest better served by desertion in spite of the severe sanctions attached to the act. Or a worker may find his personal interest better served by quitting his job and losing the pay rather than continuing to perform unsafe work. Clearly, the personal consequences of the act itself as well as the sanctions for compliance and noncompliance enter into the calculus of self-interest.

In encounters with unjust authority, there is a more subtle argument why self-interest tends to favor compliance. For illustration, we return to the workers in Fisher 1. Teefee, the foreman, is dragging little Joe Urban off to the office to fire him. Assume there is a fellow worker who believes the firing is unjust but who has a prudent concern for his self-interest. He notes that many other workers are witnessing the scene. If they intervene successfully, the injustice will be prevented and he will gain the benefit, since the prevention of injustice is a collective good which one shares whether or not one has contributed to gaining it. Self-interest dictates that one not risk one's job when one can ride free on the actions of others.

Suppose the action to impede the authority system is unsuccessful and the collective good is not produced. Then the argument for nonintervention is even stronger. The injustice continues and the risk of retaliatory action against the rebellious will probably be increased. To have intervened is to have risked one's job with nothing to show for it.

BONDS OF AUTHORITY

Beyond considerations of self-interest, there are more subtle bonds of authority. They operate to keep us complying even when no real issue of sanctions is involved.

1. Obligations to legitimate authority. It is important to recognize, as Milgram does, that authority systems exert their own moral claim for compliance. Assume, for the moment, that the authorities are seen as legitimate and acting within their domain of responsibility. In such an encounter, those who accept regulation comply, in part because they feel an obligation or duty to do so. As Milgram puts it, the moral concerns of a person in such an encounter focus on

> . . . how well he is living up to the expectations that the authority has of
> him. In wartime, a soldier does not ask whether it is good or bad to bomb

a hamlet; he does not experience shame or guilt in the destruction of a village: rather he feels pride or shame depending on how well he has performed the mission assigned to him (1974: 8).

Authorities typically operate with a presumption of legitimacy. The authority in the Milgram encounter was buttressed by the legitimating ideology of science. This ideology was institutionally embedded in Yale University, but the presumption of legitimacy was apparently still operating in his Bridgeport version. In this variation of his basic fabrication, Milgram invented a fictitious organization calling itself Research Associates of Bridgeport, which conducted the experiment in rented offices in a commercial building in the downtown shopping area of Bridgeport, Connecticut.

Even such fictitious entities as this seem able to operate on a presumption of legitimacy that allows the authority to make a moral claim on participants. This presumption is bolstered by the contractual nature of the obligation. Potential challengers have voluntarily agreed to participate and accepted payment, providing a basis for the authorities' claim that they have undertaken a commitment which they are morally obliged to honor.

Authorities may make a claim of obligation to comply, but challengers can contest this claim. The authority may be accused of usurping office by force or trickery. One has no obligation to comply with authorities that have no legitimate basis. Or authorities may be claimed to have forfeited, through malfeasance, their right to be obeyed.

One need not make such a wholesale attack on an authority system to void the obligation. Challengers may grant the authorities the right to regulate some aspects of their behavior, but put boundaries around the scope of appropriate regulation. Here, the specific obligation is voided on grounds that the authorities have overstepped their prerogatives—without challenging the authorities' general right to regulate within their scope.

There is frequently a contractual element in the claim of obligation. Those subject to regulation have entered voluntarily into an agreement that obliges them to comply. When one accepts a position in a hierarchical organization, for example, one has contracted to accept regulation within the scope of that authority system. A challenger may void the obligation by voiding this contract. Milgram's subjects frequently attempted to do this by offering to return the money they were paid for participating. The authority in this situation attempted to keep the contract in force by refusing to take the money back and insisting that the original obligation remained in force.

2. Face-work. Encounters with authority are a special case of general encounters. In all face-to-face interactions factors operate to restrain challenge, and Goffman has done the most to make us aware of them. Every social situation is built upon a working consensus among the participants. One of its chief premises is that once a definition of the situation has been projected and agreed upon by participants, there shall be no challenge to it. Disruption of the working consensus has the character of moral transgression. Open conflict about the definition of the situation is incompatible with polite exchange.

> When an individual projects a definition of the situation and then makes an implicit or explicit claim to be a person of a particular kind, he automatically exerts a moral demand upon the others, obliging them to value and treat him in the manner that persons of his kind have a right to expect (Goffman, 1959: 185).

Milgram, describing some of the factors that keep a subject complying, includes "politeness on his part, his desire to uphold his initial promise of aid to the experimenter, and the awkwardness of withdrawal" (1974: 7). To challenge authority, one must make a scene, which many people are reluctant to do. The smooth flow of interaction will be disrupted and an awkward and, perhaps unpleasant, interpersonal exchange will result.

Since the norms of polite interaction prohibit discrediting the claims of others, potential challengers run the risk of making asses of themselves. Apart from any consideration of sanctions, they may appear boorish and rude. Frequently, they may not be entirely clear about just what is happening, and the next word or action by authorities or potential challengers may make a protest or refusal seem hasty and ill-considered. Fools rush in where angels fear to tread.

These *face-work* problems are manageable ones. If it is risky to rush in with a challenge, one can reduce the risk by easing in gradually, watching the reactions of others. Potential challengers sometimes engage in a kind of verbal milling about, checking out the general mood before venturing out on a limb. Initially, accusations may be implicit, sometimes coming in the form of apparently innocent questions. "Hey, Teefee, where you going?" asked Bud Simons in conversational tone as the foreman dragged Joe Urban past him. But once the ice is broken, the risk of being embarrassed by inappropriate action has been greatly reduced.

As for the obligation to protect the face of authorities, we need to differentiate between the individual and the role. Above, we focused on voiding obligations to the authority system. Face-work focuses on the obligation to the persons within the role. Such individuals can make the job of overcoming face-work considerations easier through their actions. If they behave with arrogance and contempt toward potential challengers, few are likely to be much concerned with offering civility in return.

Agents of authority, however, are frequently civil and even friendly and affable. Kraus (1947) describes the plant manager, Evan Parker, greeting the automobile workers as "smooth as silk. 'You can smoke if you want to, boys,' he said as he bid them to take the available chairs. . . . The men were almost bowled over by this manner." Under such circumstances, face-work considerations may play an important role in maintaining compliance.

There may be no way of making a challenge without upsetting the smooth flow of polite interaction, but the claims of face-work are reduced by offering the people in authority roles a graceful line of retreat. Acts by potential challengers that recognize a separation between the individual and the agent of authority encourage the incumbent to establish some role distance. By inviting or allowing such disengagement, the conflict is made less personal, thereby reducing the force of face-work considerations.

3. Reification. Authority systems are products of human control, but this is sometimes forgotten by those who participate in them. Milgram calls this reification process "counter anthropomorphism":

> For decades psychologists have discussed the primitive tendency among men to attribute to inanimate objects and forces the qualities of the human species. A countervailing tendency, however, is that of attributing an impersonal quality to forces that are essentially human in origin as it they existed above and beyond any human agent, beyond the control of whim or human feeling. The human element behind agencies and institutions is denied (p. 8).

Authorities frequently encourage reification. As Sennett points out, "The language of bureaucratic power is often couched in the passive voice, so that responsibility is veiled" (1980: 180). Any given agent of an authority system can easily enough disclaim responsibility by passing the buck. "I'm only following the rules; I don't make them" is the classic ploy. In the process, the rules are externalized, binding the authority and participants alike, but placed beyond their control or ability to alter.

Depersonalizing the conflict may be helpful with face-work but it reinforces reification. The authorities may present themselves as mere agents of an external authority system beyond their personal ability to alter. With everyone disclaiming responsibility for the content of the authority which they exercise, it is no wonder that authority systems sometimes appear to have an external reality without human agency. The late Saul Alinsky pinpoints the problem in his *Rules for Radicals:*

> "In a complex urban society, it becomes increasingly difficult to single out who is to blame for any particular evil. There is a constant, and somewhat legitimate, passing of the buck. . . . One big problem is a constant shifting of responsibility from one jurisdiction to another—

individuals and bureaus one after another disclaim responsibility for particular conditions, attributing the authority for any change to some other force" (1972: 130–31).

Alinsky's advice is to personalize the target. In doing so one concretizes the responsibility for the exercise of authority, locating it in human actors. At the level of encounters, challengers can insist that the agent they are dealing with either accept responsibility for altering the rules or bring them in contact with someone else who will. In so doing, they disallow the claim that the rules have a reality independent of human agency.

It appears that the strategies of dealing with face-work and reification are in some tension. There frequently is a trade-off between them. An act that personalizes responsibility may enhance the force of face-work considerations. An act that depersonalizes the conflict may encourage reification of the rules. But the two aims are far from incompatible. When authorities themselves act uncivilly, there is no need to depersonalize the conflict. And one can insist on the alterability of the dictates of authority systems without turning all of its agents into devils.

In sum, breaking out of the bonds of authority is accomplished through a series of *divesting acts*—specific words or deeds that weaken one or more bonds.[2] We will focus especially on acts that void obligations to authority, while including those that overcome face-work constraints or personalize responsibility as well. Considerations of self-interest may remain, even when the bonds of authority have been severed; but aside from this, the process is completed when potential challengers no longer feel any obligation to comply, are no longer concerned about disrupting the smooth flow of interaction, and do not regard the authority system that lays its claim on them as beyond human agency. In such a state, they are psychologically free for participation in rebellious collective action.

Potential challengers reach such a state of increased readiness by a complicated process of interaction with authorities. One is not either neatly bound or free, but variously entwined at different times. Furthermore, different individuals in the encounter may be bound in varying degrees at any given moment. To see this breaking-out process in operation, we turn to the MHRC encounter.

DIVESTING ACTS IN THE MHRC ENCOUNTER

We start with some play-by-play descriptions of the breaking-out process. The first group is a late bloomer and the process is still in midstream, the breakout only partial at this point. The second group is

---

[2] We adopt here the term suggested by Coleman (1980).

a quick starter and, by the end of the strip, the bonds of authority are in shambles.

[The Coordinator reenters the room at the end of the initial, free discussion of the case of Mr. C. The group has reached the usual agreement on the issues.]

Coordinator: That was fine, but there were a couple of small problems. First, we'd like you to speak one at a time as much as possible so that it's clear on the tape. Another problem is that everybody here is taking the same point of view, and so for this next question we're going to ask Edward and David to take a point of view of someone who is offended by Mr. C.'s behavior. You don't like it and you think it's wrong and it really bothers you.

Edward: Yeah, but that's not how I feel.

Coordinator: Well, that's how we'd like it to be done.

Edward: Yeah, but is this going to be shown in court like this? I don't want to . . .

Coordinator: You see, this is . . .

Edward: This is just to bring out all sides of the discussion?

Coordinator: Right, you see this will raise all sides of the issue here.

Ruth: But why are you picking all men. Because you'd think, relating to a gas station, naturally a man's opinion would be more important than a woman's . . .

Coordinator: That's just the procedures we have. This is the way things have been set up here.

Barbara: Can they act like little old men who might be disturbed by such things, or something like that?

Coordinator: We'd like you to act like yourselves because, of course, the other people here . . .

Edward: [*interrupting*] I can't do that if I have to take the opposing view, because, I mean, this is a *joke!* If this is what the case really is, it's a *joke!*

Coordinator: Well, our procedures call for this, and I'd like you to try it. I don't think you'll find it that hard.

Carol: Can they say on camera on the videotape that "I am going to take an opposing view"?

Coordinator: [*exiting while speaking*] We just want you to proceed with the discussion.

[Those assigned to give false opinions do so, but preface their remarks with disclaimers, indicating that they are playing devil's advocate.]

[*A different group*]

Coordinator: [*handing out card with second question*] This time we'd like Richard, Mike, and Doris—we'd like you three to act as though you yourselves were genuinely offended by Mr. C.'s behavior.

Mike: Will that come out on the tape that we're acting?

Coordinator: Well, we'd like you to really put yourself in the frame of mind of someone who would be disturbed by Mr. C.'s behavior and try to present some arguments from that perspective.

Mike: But after we state that we're acting—that the three of us are acting on the tape.

Coordinator: No, when we put the tape on we just want you to come through with your opinions in a . . .

Mike: [*interrupting*] Yes, but I'd like to have on tape that I'm acting.

Coordinator: You see the point of this whole thing is that so far the discussion has been much too one-sided.

[Someone exclaims "great," there is some laughter, and two or three people start to talk at once.]

George: If you deliberately skew the sample like that then you haven't got a valid sample.

Coordinator: We're going to a variety of different communities and we'll be getting people from all over, but in this community here we know that there are people who are genuinely offended by Mr. C.'s behavior and we'd like those views to be on the tape too. So if you put yourselves in that frame of mind, I'm sure you . . .

Carol: [*interrupting*] It's not represented on the tape. That's not clear to people when you'd show it someplace that our opinions are . . .

Linda: I mean, they signed something that said, "Yes, we're being taped," but they didn't sign something that said, "Yes, we're being taped to display something—an opinion—that we may not stand with."

Coordinator: Yes, I know, but these are the procedures that we've established here and . . .

Fred: I think you're offending community standards. [*laughter in group*]

Linda: You should have established it in the statement we signed, is what you should have done.

Coordinator: Yes, well that may have been some kind of problem or it might not have been but, in any event, right now here your responsibility is to continue to . . .

Mike: [*interrupting*] My responsibility has nothing to do with that. Unless it's on the tape that I'm acting, I'm not doing it.

Coordinator: [*exiting*] Well, try to put yourself in this frame of mind and let's see if we can get some good material.

Mike: There's no way, José! [*laughter in group*]

[In the ensuing discussion, some participants do provide statements against Mr. C., prefaced by devil's advocate disclaimers in some instances.]

Rim talk. The participants in the MHRC encounter were assembled, ostensibly, to discuss the case of Mr. C. Sometimes they operated in frame, talking about the details of the case. But sometimes they turned their attention to the rim of this frame—to the surrounding context in which it was embedded. In particular, they questioned the reasons for the procedures they were being asked to follow.

The first group illustrates such rim talk.[3] The coordinator is being pushed to justify the MHRC procedures. Although he presents the procedures as external and fixed, in fact the group is successful in engaging him in a negotiation about what is expected of them.

Rim talk is a major first step in breaking out. It both undermines bonds of authority and establishes an opportunity for developing a collective orientation and adopting an injustice frame. It provides a way of easing into more rebellious actions without risking much damage to one's own or the coordinator's face. Rim talk typically begins with a relatively polite question in which accusation is only implicit.

By making procedures a matter of negotiation, rim talk attacks the claim that they are immutable. The legitimating frame begins to lose its taken-for-granted quality. And most important of all, rim talk provides the basis for future, contract-voiding actions. By making the procedures a focus of attention and forcing the coordinator to defend them, participants pave the way for further actions that deny their obligation to comply.

Early rim talk, we hypothesize, should be related to a successful rebellion career. Even the most tractable group has moments when someone raises a question about the rim of the activity in which participants are engaged. All 33 groups had rim talk before act 3, but the successful groups were earlier than the others and the tractables were conspicuously slow in producing rim talk.

It is important for a group to take this first step right away—when they are presented with the first dilemma of compliance. They are freer, then, to use the break scenes to figure out what is happening. If they have already engaged in rim talk, each new compliance dilemma provides an opportunity for reframing and organizing acts to occur.

Figure 9–1 shows support for this argument. Almost two-thirds of the groups with early rim talk succeeded, while less than one-third of the others did. Breaking out does not seem to have been a problem for the fizzlers at this point—three of the four engaged the coordinator in early rim talk. None of the tractables managed rim talk until well into the middle of act 2. Every mobilized group and mobilized factional success had rim talk in act 1, usually in the opening scene.

Contract voiding. Rim talk is an important first step, but to break out more fully, participants must engage in divesting acts that imply (or state explicitly) "I have no obligation to comply." We distinguish four such divesting acts in the MHRC encounter:

---

[3] Operationally, rim talk is defined as a strip in which the coordinator makes three separate justification efforts in succession in response to questions or objections from participants.

FIGURE 9-1   Immediate rim talk and career

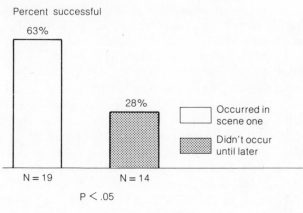

Percent successful

1. *Explicit claim that the coordinator's requests violated the contract.*   Linda did this when she told the coordinator that he was asking participants to do something that they had not agreed to. She even offered him gratuitous advice on how to redraw the contract and make it more binding for future groups.

2. *Offer to return the fee for participation.*   One way of terminating the obligation was to withdraw from the contract by returning the money that one was paid at the beginning of the session. "Sir, you can come back in here and get my $10 because I'm not doing anything on tape that I feel against," one woman told the coordinator. If there was any question of an obligation to comply, it was clearly removed by returning the money, although the coordinator's refusal to accept it may have caused continuing problems for some. This way of voiding the contract did not occur in the two examples above, but it did occur in the opening scene in three groups and in later scenes in several more.

3. *Explicit refusal to comply.*   To refuse to do what the coordinator was asking—except on grounds of incapacity—denied an obligation to comply. The coordinator typically treated a refusal as a plea of incapacity and reassured the person that what he was asking was not too difficult to perform—whenever such an interpretation was possible. But such a gambit was of no use against an explicit rejection of obligation, as in Mike's statement: "My responsibility has nothing to do with that."

4. *Threat to walk out.*   This did not occur in the quoted transcripts, but it did occur in act 1 in three groups and in several more groups in act 2.

There were, then, four different specific divesting acts that participants in the MHRC encounter employed to void the obligation to comply. Any time one of these occurred, it was an important *collective* event in the life of the group. An *individual* had to perform the act, but it was a public act. Everyone witnessed the occurrence of the specific divesting act, whether or not they supported it. At this point, the observer may not have been asked to give false opinions and, hence, was not yet being pressed into complicity but a blow had been struck against any future claim of obligation.

Early contract voiding has an especially strong relationship to a successful career. As Figure 9–2 shows, more than three-quarters of the groups which broke out to this degree in act 1 were successful. If such divesting acts had not occurred before the final scenes of act 2, it was almost too late. Only 2 of 10 such groups eventually succeeded. Factional successes and fizzlers were somewhat slower than successful groups, but tractables were by far the slowest. None of them had contract-voiding acts by the middle of act 2, and, for the most part, they seemed to carry the bonds of authority through the entire encounter.

FIGURE 9–2   Contract voiding and career

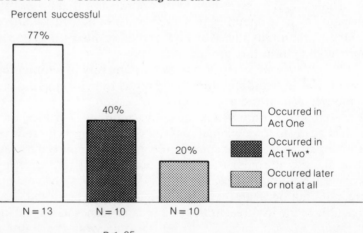

Percent successful

77%

40%

20%

N = 13   N = 10   N = 10

☐ Occurred in Act One

▓ Occurred in Act Two*

▒ Occurred later or not at all

P< .05

* To qualify, it must occur before the final break scene.

One deviant case is worth noting. There was only one successful group in which no contract-voiding acts occurred before the affidavit scene. If the process of breaking out must be completed before a group can succeed in achieving collective resistance, how was this late bloomer able to make it anyway?

The most striking thing about this group was its heavy use of protest humor and irony. As we argued earlier, these devices help a group build solidarity and act more easily as a unit. Although the participants did not resist the coordinator openly before the affidavit, they engaged him in rim talk almost immediately and greeted his justifications with derisive laughter on several occasions. They had little disagreement among themselves but didn't seem to get really serious about the situation until confronted with the affidavit. Then, they had a protracted discussion and argument with the coordinator and eventually reached a group consensus that no one would sign. Apparently, this group was so advanced in the process of working together that they were able to overcome the handicap of not having broken out very thoroughly before this point.

PERSONAL ATTACKS ON THE COORDINATOR

We argued above for the double-edged nature of personalizing the conflict. By holding the coordinator personally responsible, the group countered his attempts at reification but they increased the damage to his face. The coordinator was distant and made no play for sympathy but he never raised his voice or attacked participants. In contrast, he was sometimes made the target of ridicule for his apparent moral obtuseness. He sometimes got flustered and there can be little doubt that the participants perceived when they were giving him a hard time. The face-work forces for compliance were strengthened when people began feeling sorry for the coordinator in his unfortunate job. If he was just a poor soul trying to do an unpleasant job, why not go along with what he asked to spare him further humiliation? We did not have too many instances of overt expressions of personal hostility toward the coordinator, but it is worth examining the few for insight on this issue.

The personal hostility expressed toward the coordinator before act 3 in nine groups had no relationship to their rebellion careers. Five groups were successful and the others included a factional success, two fizzlers, and a tractable. If we look at the interaction immediately following this expression, there is some evidence of at least a short-run negative effect. In four of the nine cases, the group experienced internal disagreement shortly afterward, usually sparked by someone in the group advocating compliance. In four groups there was no change and in only one group was there an achievement of a new level of rebellion during the rest of the scene. Apparently, personal hostility expressed to the coordinator led some participants to begin defending the coordinator or, at least, looking for some way out of an apparent impasse. The net result often was increased conflict within the group.

SELF-INTEREST CONSIDERATIONS IN THE
MHRC ENCOUNTER

Concern with gaining inducements and avoiding constraints existed in subtle form in the MHRC encounter. On the constraint side, a number of participants mentioned, during the debriefing, a concern that the coordinator might have demanded his money back if they had refused to comply. Various divesting acts could affect such a concern. If someone offers the money back and the coordinator refuses to accept it, this clearly indicates that the coordinator is not going to press such a demand. When a participant explicitly refuses to comply and the coordinator uses no sanctions, again such a concern should be diminished. Hence, the contract-voiding acts above also undermine the fear of this negative sanction.

Some participants had inducements on their mind at various points. Earning money was the primary motive for being there for most of them, and many recalled that a series of projects had been mentioned at the time they were recruited. In the debriefing, some of them indicated their hope that they would be asked back to participate in other projects to earn additional money, and their fear that they would have jeopardized this opportunity by being uncooperative. Although the coordinator never suggested this possibility, if it were on someone's mind, none of the divesting acts neutralized it and it undoubtedly continued to be a force for compliance for some.

In some groups, participants expressed concern about their legal liability if they provided false testimony. Whenever such a concern was expressed or suggested, the coordinator reassured participants that the MHRC assumed all legal liability. "Don't worry," he would say. "It is perfectly clear that these are our procedures and we're responsible for them. You have nothing to worry about." In fact, the coordinator sometimes offered such reassurance when participants were not really expressing self-concern. It is unlikely that the fear of negative sanctions by outside agencies played any significant role in the MHRC encounter.

WHO WAS DIVESTING?

Again we explore the characteristics of the individuals who engaged in divesting acts to see if they had distinctive attitudes or experiences. We focus on those exemplars who were first or second in a group to engage in contract-voiding acts.[4] There were 61 such individuals in the 28 groups in which it occurred, and only 4 of them were planted mobilizing agents. Ironically, in the exemplar variations, our confederate turned up as an exemplar only once, but lagged behind spontaneous exemplars in the others.

We compared exemplars to the rest of the sample on all of our

---

[4] Since there were four different kinds of contract-voiding acts, it was possible to have more than two exemplars in a group and a few groups did produce as many as three exemplars.

questionnaire measures of attitudes and attributes and found few distinctive characteristics.[5] Again, there was no difference in education, or in our measures of organizational and political experience. Women were again overrepresented, but this time only slightly so, and the difference was not statistically significant. Only one attitude question differentiated the exemplars. Participants were asked, "Generally speaking, how much do you think we can trust the government in Washington to do what is right?" Only 17 percent of the exemplars, but half of the rest of the sample, gave a high trust response on this item. Perhaps such general skepticism about authority systems makes it easier to break the bonds when the unjust variety is encountered.

There was no particular tension between contract voiding and speaking for the group. Indeed, we found a heavy overlap among the individuals performing these acts. More than half of the spokespersons were also exemplars.

SUMMARY

Rebellion, we have argued, is a rare event, partly because of the sanctioning power of authorities and the self-interest of potential challengers in compliance. Even when sanctions are not especially relevant, participants feel bound by social-psychological and moral forces to comply. These bonds include the duty or obligation to comply, face-work, and reification. One breaks these bonds by specific divesting acts that void obligation to authority, manage face-work and personalize responsibility.

In the MHRC encounter, we focused on the early achievement of rim talk and four types of contract-voiding acts. Both variables were related to a successful career in the MHRC encounter. The most successful groups established rim talk at the time of the first dilemma of compliance and had contract voiding by the end of act 1. Tractables, in particular, showed a failure to divest the coordinator.

The freer a group felt from the obligation to comply, the more easily it could proceed successfully with other processes. It was difficult for a group to develop a collective orientation when some members still felt obliged to do what the coordinator was asking. It was difficult to confront the coordinator with a divesting act when one felt incomplete and partial group support. Finally, it was hard to feel completely free of the bonds of authority if one were still confused and unsure about what was happening, a process we consider in the next chapter.

---

[5] We have relatively complete information on 50 of the exemplars, the rest being participants from trial runs.

Adopting an injustice frame | 10

We mustn't forget the most obvious reason why people allow their behavior to be regulated by authorities. Frequently, they believe that what they are being asked to do is utterly innocuous, if not benign. Those who obediently form a line at an usher's request aren't mindless sheep. "First come, first served" is an honored and accepted principle to follow in providing a service. A line is a well-known, generally effective mechanism for implementing that principle. By using his authority to provide this mechanism, the usher is producing a collective benefit for the participants: they are provided with an efficient and fair way of gaining admission to a theater instead of being left to push and shove.

What we have just described above is a *legitimating frame* for the usher in his encounter with movie patrons. We don't suggest, of course, that the people complying with his request are consciously thinking in such terms. On the contrary, the frame has a taken-for-granted quality. Nothing they are asked to do calls the legitimating frame into question. If the usher insisted on beginning the line with the late arrivals—operating on a first-come, last-served principle—the legitimating frame might well come explicitly to the surface. Various participants would denounce the procedure as unfair, and the legitimating frame would become a matter of conscious attention.

If an authority is acting in a normal, unexceptionable manner, then, the underlying legitimating frame is taken for granted. But sometimes actions or events occur that break the hegemony of the legitimating frame by calling into question one or more of its elements. Not all quarrels with authorities call the legitimating frame into question. One might believe that agents of some authority system are clumsy and incompetent in performing their designated tasks, for example.

The type of quarrel that concerns us here goes deeper. An *injustice frame* is an interpretation of what is happening that supports the conclusion that an authority system is violating the shared moral principles of the participants. An alternative to the legitimating frame, it provides a reason for noncompliance.

Participants may be looking for a reason. Authorities may be acting in ways that provoke suspicion, hostility, and anger. There is good evidence, as Zajonc has argued, that such feelings may precede a coherent interpretation of what is happening and guide the search for meaning. "Preferences need no inferences" is Zajonc's epigram to make the point. "Affective reactions can occur without extensive perceptual and cognitive encoding, are made with greater confidence than cognitive judgments, and can be made sooner" (1980: 151).

The bonds of authority discussed in the last chapter are primarily affective bonds. With the legitimating frame implicit and taken for granted, they provide an unanalyzed feeling that one ought to comply. The cognitive process of adopting an injustice frame is complementary to breaking out. It provides a rationale for acting on the hostility or anger that participants may feel. These feelings, in turn, animate their suspicion, lead them to seek certain information, and alert them to flaws in the legitimating frame.

The adoption of an injustice frame in place of a legitimating frame as a context of meaning for what is happening is an important part of the process by which a group of potential challengers mobilize. Turner and Killian suggest that "a movement is inconceivable apart from a vital sense that some established practice or mode of thought is wrong and ought to be replaced. . . . People express discontent, complain, and even engage in impulsive resistance to conditions. But the discovery that their complaints are really expressions of injustice requires that the new terms be formulated . . ." (1972: 259, 265). Moore agrees: "Any political movement against oppression has to develop a new diagnosis and remedy for existing forms of suffering, a diagnosis and remedy by which this suffering stands morally condemned. These new moral standards of condemnation constitute the core identity of any oppositional movement" (1978: 88).

People do not necessarily choose between the legitimating frame and the injustice frame, but may hold both to some degree, wavering back and forth. Piven and Cloward point out that "people seek to legitimate what they do, even when they are defiant, and the authority of elites to define what is legitimate remains powerful, even during periods of stress and disorder" (1977: 14). It is useful to think of the frames that individuals hold as a vector with weights for the competing frames that vary over time. The weights represent the degree of conviction or subjective probability that the given frame is operative at any given moment in an encounter.

We need a language to express the degree of conviction attached to any given frame. One *entertains* the injustice frame if the interpretation has crossed one's mind, but is seen as improbable; *considers* the injustice frame if is taken seriously as a possibility but it is not regarded as probable; *adopts* the injustice frame if one regards it as more plausible than the legitimating frame as an interpretation of what is happening.[1]

But the adoption of an injustice frame involves more than a series of individuals privately adopting a different frame for interpreting what is happening. For collective adoption of an injustice frame, it must be shared by the potential challengers in a public way. This allows the participants to realize not only that they share the injustice frame, but that everyone in the group is aware that it is shared.

REFRAMING ACTS

A *reframing act* is any word or deed by a challenger that furthers the collective adoption of an injustice frame. The adoption of an injustice frame generally takes time, and is rarely compressed into a single encounter. Heirich's sensitivity to such issues in his description of the Berkeley free speech movement provides us with an unusually detailed account of the process in operation.

Two days before the seizure of the police car, a campus socialist organization heard a speech by Hal Draper. Draper's speech drew a fair-sized crowd, perhaps because his topic was "Clark Kerr's View of the University as a Factory." Kerr, the president of the university, had written a book, *The Uses of the University*, that provided a legitimating ideology for the institution. Draper's talk attacked Kerr's view of the university and apparently offered participants in the ongoing free speech controversy needed ammunition.

The day after Draper's speech there was a confrontation between officials from the dean's office and people who had set up tables displaying political literature in the forbidden area. A crowd gathered, and some of the participants stood on chairs to address the group. Jack Weinberg, one of the speakers, gives this description of what was going through his mind:

> Mario [Savio] spoke for a while pointing out what was happening. This was the first speech of the Free Speech Movement. When Mario got

---

[1] Translating these terms into the language of a probability vector, one might define them as follows, where P_I is the weight of the injustice frame: entertain = $0 < P_I \leq .1$; consider = $.1 < P_I \leq .5$; adopt = $P_I > .5$.

down, I was the second person that spoke. . . . I remember my speech at
the time—two things I recall: the night before, Hal Draper had given a
talk at Stiles on "Clark Kerr's View of the University as a Factory." . . . I
was at this talk, and Mario was also there for at least part of his talk. At
the time I felt I was greatly influenced by this speech. I talked about the
University factory. I was essentially trying to fit some of what was happening into the theoretical framework—explaining it in terms of this
framework that had been exposited the night before. At the time I felt I
was very heavily dependent on the speech. [Heirich, 1971: 123.]

That evening, Savio made a speech in which he drew on Draper's
argument in articulating an injustice frame:

I'm suggesting legally, therefore, that the distinction that they make
between students and nonstudents has no basis except harassment. . . .
Furthermore, they claim that the university is neutral. A lot of hogwash!
It's *legally* neutral. It's the most un-politically-neutral organization that
I've had personal contact with. It's really an institution that serves the
interests and represents the Establishment of the United States. And we
have Clark Kerr's word on it in his book on the multiversity.

As I said before, the purpose of the university is simple: it's to create a
product. The product is to fit into certain factories. You go out and take
part in the Establishment and that's why there is a university.

Anybody who wants to say anything on this campus, just like anybody
on the city street, should have the right to do so—and no concessions by
the bureaucracy should be acceded to by us, should be considered by us,
until they include complete freedom of speech! [Heirich, 1971: 135.]

The capture of the police car occurred the following day. The adoption of an injustice frame was already underway, and this new encounter presented opportunities for its further articulation and diffu-
sion as protestors spoke from the roof of the police car. Indeed, Draper
spoke at this impromptu rally, again likening the university to a factory
and explaining what had just happened in terms of this model.

Heirich's discussion suggests a useful distinction between two types
of reframing acts.

1. *Attention calling.* Attention-calling acts are words or deeds that
point to something questionable in what the authority is doing or
about to do in the encounter. "This fellow's under arrest!" Savio
shouted to the crowd as he came upon the scene in Sproul Plaza while
Weinberg was being taken to the police car. The attention calling act
says to other participants in the encounter: "Look at what's happening
here." Something out of the ordinary, requiring attention, is going on
or about to occur.

2. *Context setting.* Context-setting acts identify or define what is
wrong by applying an injustice frame to what is happening in the

encounter. Those who stood on the police car, for example, and explained what was happening to the crowd, presented a model of the university that gave meaning to the arrest as the operation of unjust authority. An interpretation may have several parts, and any given context-setting act may focus only on a limited aspect.

Reframing, then, is accomplished through a series of specific words or deeds that promote the collective adoption of an injustice frame. More specifically, it is accomplished through public acts that call attention to something questionable in what the authority is doing, and link it to an injustice frame. When participants come to share an injustice frame, they are in a state of heightened readiness for rebellious collective action.

It takes time for a group to reach this state. As the process unfolds, the degree of credence that any participant gives the injustice frame fluctuates as challengers and authorities interact. Furthermore, acceptance of the injustice frame at any given moment may vary widely from person to person. The MHRC encounter compressed this process into the course of a single encounter; we return to it to examine the reframing process in operation.

REFRAMING ACTS IN THE MHRC ENCOUNTER

The explicit part of the legitimating frame for the MHRC encounter was expressed in the covering letter. The MHRC, a legitimate business enterprise, provided services to other businesses. It was following standard professional procedures in carrying out its work and paying above-average compensation to participants. Other parts of the legitimating frame were implicit: the coordinator had an employer's right to define what the task at hand was, and the participants had the obligation to perform these tasks conscientiously.

The hegemony of this legitimating frame is well illustrated in the long prologue before act 1 begins. Participants were asked, for example, to fill out a brief questionnaire giving their opinions on a number of public issues. Everyone complied. Indeed, anyone not complying would have been considered peculiar by the other participants. They agreed to participate in research on community standards and the filling out of the questionnaire was an ordinary, unexceptionable request. The legitimating frame was operative; it was taken for granted by participants, and the coordinator was not called upon to justify it.

But the MHRC's legitimating frame was fragile. Once individuals began privately to entertain an injustice frame, they moved rather quickly to suggest it to others for public consideration. Once it was considered, additional provocations by the coordinator could be interpreted in terms of this injustice frame. Many groups had collectively adopted it by the time the coordinator introduced the affidavit for their signatures at the beginning of act 3.

The content of the injustice frame in the MHRC encounter can be stated simply enough. The MHRC was working, on behalf of its oil company client, to suborn perjury. It was collecting material that could be edited in a manner that would distort the true nature of community standards in a legal proceeding—to the detriment of the unfortunate Mr. C. The injustice frame provided a context within which the coordinator's acts made sense—that is, he was acting as the agent of an unjust authority.

To a clued-in outside observer, this injustice frame may have seemed like a natural and obvious one to adopt. It was a good deal less obvious to the naive participants. The scenario unfolded gradually; it took time to put the pieces together. Meanwhile, the coordinator was pressing participants to get on with their assigned task. The clues were there in abundance, but they were not necessarily obvious.

A good many participants already had negative feelings toward the MHRC, even before the first dilemma of compliance. The appeal, in the covering letter, to "contribute to the continued strength of the free enterprise system" did not rouse the spirit of all participants. More important, the MHRC was representing an oil company that had invaded the privacy of, and then fired, the innocent Mr. C. If one judges companies by the company they keep, the MHRC had poor companions. Some of the participants, feeling at least mild hostility toward the MHRC even before the first dilemma of compliance, were primed for an alternative to the legitimating frame.

There were also many participants who were not so ready to call the legitimating frame into question. They were not equally receptive to information that would suggest an alternative. For a heterogeneous group to reach the point where they share the injustice frame, questionable acts by authorities must be called to everyone's attention, and the elements of the injustice frame must be publicly articulated. One can see this reframing process in operation in the following transcripts.

[It is the beginning of act 2, and the first group, a fizzler, has been compliant up to this point. The coordinator has just told the group that there will be a short break and has left the room. A number of fragmentary conversations are going on simultaneously. Fred has been expressing some private concern to Thelma, who is sitting next to him.]

Thelma: This won't have any bearing on you.

Fred: It's not going to have any bearing on me, but it will have a bearing on Mr. C.

[Thelma gets an idea and starts checking the MHRC cover letter lying on the table. Meanwhile, another conversation goes on among other people about the case. Thelma finds what she is looking for and gets the attention of the group.]

Thelma: This is what they're trying to do, see. [*reading*] "We feel that in this way we can contribute to the continued strength of the free enterprise system." So this MHRC is a private thing. What they're trying to do is be on these big oil companies' side.

Lisa: Right.

Thelma: So they're trying to kick Mr. C. out, right.

[*"Yeah," "Right," murmurs of assent from several people.*]

[The second group, a factional success, has also been compliant to this point. Again it is the beginning of act 2, shortly after the coordinator has introduced the first break scene and exited. Various private side conversations are going on until John addresses the group.]

John: I came here on the assumption that they just wanted us to give our opinions. I mean, we're not a jury . . .

Carol: The oil company wants to find out how much of a case they have in selecting a jury.

Dan: The thing is, our opinions are false. If we're not giving our real beliefs, we're giving a false impression.

Tom: Right, and he said that this will be shown in court.

Carol: We need to put a statement in front, saying like, "It's not really my opinion." Otherwise, it's not fair, it's not really your opinion.

Tom: Otherwise, we're going to be inadvertently screwing Mr. C.

Carol: Yeah, conceivably.

Jane: Well, I certainly hope Mr. C. wins.

[*They return to discussing issues in the case.*]

[The third group, a late bloomer, has also been relatively compliant through most of act 1, but begins the reframing process before the break scene that marks the opening of act 2. This group is one of the variations with an implanted organizer, who makes some contribution in the dialogue that follows. A compliant discussion of the case is going on while Gloria and George are having a whispered side conversation. During a pause in the discussion, Gloria speaks up.]

Gloria: We'll abstain over here. We don't like to do it this way. I don't think we should do this—taking opposite points of view. This is this guy, if this is all for real, you know. We can't sit here and say something we don't believe and . . .

George: This isn't an "as if" case. It's real.

Gloria: Yeah, this is real.

Tom: I think you're right.

Dan: We could start it with a statement that says, "This is not my point of view."

Gloria: They could just cut that out.

George: Yeah.

Organizer: There is something awfully funny about this.

> [At this point, the group begins discussing issues in the case again. Shortly thereafter, the coordinator enters and, and after an exchange in which various members of the group ask for justifications of procedures, he exits for the first break scene.]

Organizer: It seems to me that there's something wrong with this process . . .

Gloria: [*interrupting*] I've never seen anything like this before!

George: This is pretty crooked.

Organizer: They're asking us to lie in front of the camera, and I can't believe that's a proper procedure for tapes that are going to be presented in court.

> [One of the participants interjects a question about what people were told at the time of recruiting, and they establish that they were told that the purpose of the project was to study public opinion.]

Gloria: This isn't public opinion, because we're giving false opinion.

Arthur: I disagree with giving false opinions. We're taking it too lightly when he asks us to lie. It says right here [*indicating covering letter*] that what we're dealing with is a human life. When he asks us to lie . . .

Jane: This is this guy's job. He's spending a lot of money to go to court for this and he deserves to win.

Organizer: They haven't given us any kind of guarantee that this won't be edited and cut up. We don't know what's going to happen with these tapes.

We are sometimes asked whether the participants were really concerned about the fate of Mr. C. or merely about being asked to lie. The question, we submit, is misleading since the distinction is not really a meaningful one for the participants. The court case of Mr. C. is an integral part of the injustice frame, making the giving of false opinions an act of complicity. Remove the injustice context and the act takes on a different meaning. Imagine, for example, that the coordinator had asked participants to take the opinion of someone offended by Mr. C.'s behavior, but had put the request in a different context, indicating that the research involved a study of persuasive communication. Giving false opinions would no longer be seen as lying, but merely as role playing.

Evidence bearing on this point appears in the questionnaire that participants filled out after knowledge of the hoax. They were asked to indicate on a seven-point scale how much they were bothered by a series of things about the MHRC during the course of the encounter, reflecting the different elements of the injustice frame.

As Table 10–1 indicates, they were bothered by all elements, with little or no distinction. Eighty-five percent of them were bothered by the fact that the MHRC and the oil company seemed out to get Mr. C.,

TABLE 10–1 Adoption of different elements of the injustice frame*

Objectives	Percent bothered
People were told to give opinions that they didn't believe in.	85%
False evidence could be presented in court.	92
The videotapes could be edited.	82
The oil company and the MHRC were "out to get" Mr. C.	85

* Number involved: 182.

the same overwhelming percentage as were bothered by being told to give opinions they rejected. These are not separable concerns, but elements in an integrated injustice frame. According to the participants' post hoc accounts, the injustice frame in all elements was adopted by the majority of participants in all groups by the end of act 3.

This data may exaggerate the collective adoption at the beginning of the final act. Some groups reached the affidavit scene with unresolved questions about what was happening. While a few of the participants had pretty much adopted the injustice frame, a few others were merely willing to consider it. The doubters were unconvinced that the MHRC could get away with its scheme, even if one granted its intent. Such differences were often reflected in late disagreements about how to respond to the dilemmas of compliance.

Shared adoption, when it occurred, resulted from the two kinds of reframing utterances described above:

1. *Attention calling.* We include here all claims that something out of the ordinary was happening, requiring attention. More specifically, we are looking for claims that people were giving a false impression of their opinions, that the videotapes could be edited, or that false evidence could be presented in court. Numerous examples appear in the transcripts quoted above.

An attention-calling act means, at a minimum, that someone is ready to consider an injustice frame. Sometimes a person who was entertaining this frame would test the waters with a private comment to a neighbor before offering it to the group. This is exactly what happens in the exchange introduced by Gloria and George in the third transcript cited above. By offering the comment publicly, Gloria gives others who may have been entertaining similar ideas an invitation to jump in and consider them more seriously, thus moving the group a step closer to adopting an injustice frame.

All 33 groups had attention-calling acts before the affidavit scene.

The legitimating frame never survived act 2 without challenge, even among tractables and fizzlers. As usual, there were advantages for beginning this process early, at the first dilemma of compliance. As Figure 10–1 shows, two-thirds of the groups that had attention calling in the opening scene went on to success, while less than 40 percent of the others achieved this benchmark. Attention calling was clearly far from sufficient for success, but it set the reframing process in motion.

FIGURE 10–1   Immediate attention calling and career

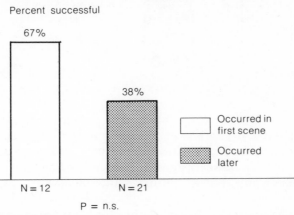

Percent successful

67%

38%

☐ Occurred in first scene

▦ Occurred later

N = 12   N = 21

P = n.s.

2. Context setting.   We include here those remarks that linked the giving of false opinions with an injustice to Mr. C. They made the injustice frame explicit by pointing to the unfair consequences for Mr. C. that might result from compliance. "So, they're trying to kick Mr. C. out," observes one participant in the first group quoted above. "We're going to be inadvertently screwing Mr. C." says a participant in the second group. "This is this guy's job," says a participant in the third group.

Context-setting acts made clear the issue of complicity by linking compliance in the encounter with an injustice. The two break scenes, free of the usual pressures from the coordinator to perform a task, provided a golden opportunity for context setting—but not all groups took advantage of the opportunity.

Slightly more than half of the groups did context setting before act 3. The relationship to rebellion career was particularly strong when context calling occurred by the middle of act 2, before the last break scene in which a group was left free to discuss strategy. As Figure 10–2 shows, three-fourths of the groups that had context setting by this point succeeded, compared to one-third of the others.

FIGURE 10–2 **Early context setting and career**

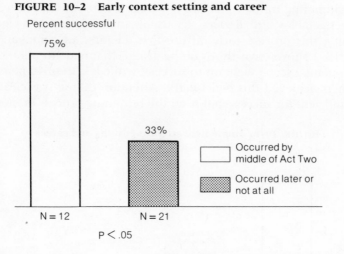

Percent successful

75%

33%

☐ Occurred by
middle of Act Two

▦ Occurred later or
not at all

N = 12   N = 21

P < .05

Groups that had the earliest and most complete reframing acts were most successful in their rebellion careers. Only four groups did context setting in act 1; all were successes. Only six groups had both immediate attention calling and context setting by the middle of act 2; all were successes.

There was also a very strong relationship between context setting and mobilization activity, as Figure 10–3 shows. Here, we include the three factional successes along with the nine successful groups that prepared for future action. Almost two thirds of the groups with context-setting acts had later mobilizing activity, while only one of the 16 without context setting prepared for future action.

As usual, it is instructive to look closely at the exception. This group, one of the trial runs, was endowed not only with a planted mobilizing agent, but also, by chance, with an outspoken participant who reacted at once when the coordinator introduced the first compliance dilemma. Although he was not asked to give false opinions, he urged others not to comply. The planted mobilizing agent remained silent during this exchange, and the other participants rejected the advice. A more prolonged exchange with the coordinator didn't occur until the end of act 1, and a number of attention-calling comments were made during the first break scene. The group became quite rebellious during act 2, but still made no public articulation of the injustice frame.

When the affidavit was presented to this group at the beginning of act 3, there was strong, unanimous resistance. The group prepared for further action and seized the participation agreements as well. This group appeared to have suffered an initial gap in shared consciousness, attributable in part to the failure in context setting. The early rebel was

FIGURE 10-3   Context setting and mobilization

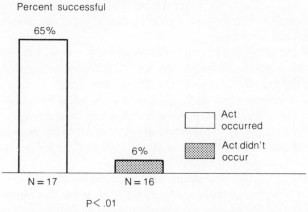

Percent successful

65%

6%

N = 17   N = 16

P< .01

* Includes nine successful groups and three factional successes with
preparation for future action.

too far in front of the rest of the group, inviting them to actions that
seemed premature without the appropriate reframing. The other participants at first declined to support him, although, by act 2, the planted
mobilizing agent was giving his full support. But events conspired to
remove the gap as the coordinator's behavior offered post hoc justification for the premature rebellion, and the group finally came together.
The injustice frame remained merely implicit throughout. This group's
ability to achieve collective resistance and other mobilizing activity
without explicit context setting remains as negative evidence for our
argument.

WHO WAS REFRAMING?

Who were the individuals leading the group toward adoption of the
injustice frame? Did these *framers* have distinctive attitudes and attributes? To explore this question, we focus on context setting.[2]

There were only 23 such framers in the 17 groups where context
setting occurred, and two of them were planted mobilizing agents.
Three others were in the 9 trial runs for which we have incomplete
information, leaving us only 18 or 19 cases for most comparisons.
Again, the most striking result was the absence of almost any distinguishing characteristics. One might expect that framers would be
higher in education, for example, but there was virtually no difference;
39 percent of the framers and 35 percent of the rest of the sample had

---

[2] More precisely, framers are defined as the first or second person in a group to
engage in context setting before act 3.

four or more years of college. Slightly more than half of the framers were women. Indeed, one is struck by their heterogeneity. One was a security guard with less than a ninth grade education; another had a social work master's degree.

Nor did framers have very distinctive attitudes. Only one item shows a significant difference: 39 percent of the framers responded "almost never" to the item, "Generally speaking, how much do you think we can trust the government in Washington to do what is right?" Only 13 percent of the rest of the sample had such a low trust response. As with contract voiding, low trust seemed to serve as an early-warning device that helped one to pick up what was happening more quickly in encounters with unjust authority.

The roles of framer, exemplar, and spokesperson were complementary rather than competitive. Most of the framers (62 percent) were also exemplars. Six of our participants were triple threats: exemplar-framer-spokespersons. The six showed no special attributes or attitudes on our questionnaire that would distinguish them from others. It is worth noting that two of these triple threats appeared in the same group—the rebellious conservatives, described in chapter 6, who managed a successful rebellion career in spite of an especially unfavorable climate.

THE HOAX FRAME

It is time to consider the perplexing issue of suspicion. So far, we have treated the framing issue as a contest between the legitimating and injustice frames. But consider a more radical shift: what is happening is not primary, untransformed activity, but a deliberately staged hoax.

One might think that the *hoax frame* is relevant only for fabrications, but this is not so. Sometimes people consider or even adopt the hoax frame when it doesn't fit. Recently, for example, we were told of a meeting of professional social workers in Berkeley that was interrupted with a public address announcement that a bomb threat had been received. The bomb, the caller indicated, was scheduled to explode at 4:00 P.M. The chairman of the meeting, being an old Berkeley resident and accustomed to such happenings, casually observed that it was only 2:30, that the threat was very probably a false alarm, and that in any event, the meeting could safely continue until 3:30. He then proceeded with the business of the day.

By 3 o'clock, some of the participants had begun to grow uneasy. Side conversations started among some of them, and they considered the possibility that they were unwittingly part of an elaborate experimental hoax. Ultimately, group members insisted on evacuating the building, deciding that, as in many such cases, it was wisest to act as if there were no hoax. Such an incident demonstrates that it is quite possible for the hoax frame to be considered or adopted even when the encounter is unfabricated.

In fabrications, of course, the hoax frame is much more likely to arise. Even the best of fabrications may not fully contain the participants. Subtle incongruities may allow leakage and, once having entertained the possibility of a hoax, the participants may begin to test their suspicions on other people or checkout various parts of the rim. For example, in the MHRC encounter, they may have scrutinized the information in the covering letter, or examined the video equipment more closely.

Suspicion was definitely a factor in the MHRC encounter despite our best efforts to contain the participants. Two separate issues were relevant here: the degree of suspicion that existed in the MHRC encounter, and how suspicion might have affected rebellion career. On the post-questionnaire, we asked participants, "Did you ever suspect that the Manufacturers' Human Relations Consultants (MHRC) was not what it claimed to be? If you suspect this, what made you suspicious and when was this?" This question invoked more than the hoax frame, since some participants responded that they suspected that the MHRC was underhandedly trying to get Mr. C.—an invocation of the injustice frame.

A number of participants replied that they suspected a psychology experiment or a test of some sort.[3] We suggest that such a post hoc measure of suspicion indicates only whether or not the respondent entertained the hoax frame. Imagine that at one point in the middle of act 2, the thought crossed your mind that you might be involved in an experimental hoax. You didn't mention it to the other participants and you didn't consider it further. Yet, when you are told that it *was* a hoax, you are likely to exclaim, "I *knew* it!" and to mention this suspicion on the postquestionnaire. If participants didn't even acknowledge suspicion after being told of the hoax, it seems fair to infer that they never entertained the hoax frame. Thus we have an outer limit on the degree of suspicion. By this measure, about one-sixth of the participants mentioned suspicion of an experimental hoax. The figure tends to be highest for Ann Arbor groups, and does not include the first six trial runs in which suspicion was substantially higher.

Some participants publicly suggested the hoax frame during the scenario. Sometimes the suggestion was made in a joking manner,

---

[3] Incidentally, no one ever blew the cover of our planted mobilizing agent. Further, several people who have watched the videotapes, knowing that one of the participants was a confederate but not knowing his precise role, have been unable to identify him correctly on the first guess.

with the speaker indicating that he did not expect to be taken seriously. For example, in one group, before the coordinator had even introduced the covering letter, some participants grew impatient waiting for late arrivals. "Maybe this is an experiment to see how long we're willing to wait here," one person joked. In another group, in the middle of a tense scene, a participant exclaimed in exasperation, "I can't believe this. We must be on Candid Camera," but no one took her literally. We took such utterances to mean that the speaker was entertaining the hoax frame, but before inferring it was considered by the group, we required that it be taken seriously by other participants. In other words, to say that a group considered the hoax frame, we required a suspicion exchange in which two or more people indicated they considered the hoax frame a serious possibility.

By such a measure, eight groups considered the hoax frame. If this figure seems high, it is mitigated by two factors. Four of the groups were in the six earliest trial runs, and it occurred only four times in the remaining 27 groups. Furthermore, the consideration usually came very late—during the lull while the group was waiting for the coordinator to phone his home office for instructions on how to deal with their refusal to sign the affidavits.

Even when the hoax frame was considered earlier than this, it was always shunted aside while the group continued to act as if they believed they were engaged in primary, untransformed activity. Only two groups, both from early trial runs, eventually adopted the hoax frame. Both adoptions came late in act 3 and were helped along by a number of leaks in the fabrication. One group considering the hoax frame began examining the equipment more closely, and discovered "University of Michigan" stenciled on the videotape deck. In another group, there was leakage in the recruiting, with some of the participants being told by an intermediary that he understood the research to be a sociology department project. During act 3, this group clearly adopted the hoax frame, even guessing that their willingness to comply was being assessed. Once a group reached this point, we made no further effort to keep the fabrication going, but moved right into the debriefing. Fortunately, adoption of the hoax frame never became a problem after the trial runs, and it is worth noting that it was never even considered in any of the groups run outside of Ann Arbor.

The hoax frame and rebellion career.   For our purposes, a hoax frame is a contaminating factor that complicates our interpretation of what happened. The implications of the hoax frame for compliance and rebellion are double-edged. If one believes that Mr. C. doesn't really exist, then one is not really being complicit in an injustice—so why make a fuss? Some participants who harbor such a suspicion may decide to lay back and watch the scenario unfold, going along with what they are being asked to do. On the other hand, if the encounter is a test of how people will react and it has no real-life consequences, then some may throw caution to the winds and, free of inhibitions, give full vent to their righteous indignation. Hence, suspicion of a hoax does not clearly bolster either compliance or rebellion.

This is part of our reason for arguing that, in the end, suspicion does not significantly affect rebellion career. Faced with the possibility of the injustice frame or the hoax frame and uncertain of the latter, participants will choose to act as if the injustice frame applied. Sometimes their logic is explicit, with someone pointing out that if the injustice frame is applicable, then they shouldn't comply; but if it is a hoax, then still no harm will be done by resistance. Participants act on the prudent principle: if in doubt, operate with the injustice frame.

SUMMARY

We have argued that, for a successful rebellion career, groups must begin reframing early, setting in motion the process of adopting an injustice frame. They do this through framing acts that call attention to something questionable in the coordinator's exercise of authority, and give his acts meaning in terms of the injustice frame.

The adoption of the injustice frame by the end of act 2 made the presentation of the affidavit a highly provocative act. The announcement on this form that "the tapes will be edited in such a way as to facilitate their presentation to the Court" was a confirming event for the injustice frame—a virtual admission by the MHRC that the fears voiced by some group members were well-grounded.

All groups engaged in attention-calling acts before the end of act 2, but the ones that did it immediately, in the opening scene, were most likely to be successful. Context setting was rarer and later, and was more strongly related to success, especially if it occurred by the middle of act 2. With one exception, groups that failed to engage in context setting also failed to mobilize for future action against the MHRC.

For a successful career, adopting an injustice frame must keep pace with the other central processes. An injustice frame by itself was insufficient for success if a group failed to develop a collective orientation and break the bonds of authority. But a shared adoption of the injustice frame helped a group to justify its noncompliance, arrive at a coordinated response to the affidavit, and recognize the necessity for future action to stop the MHRC's shenanigans.

Luck and skill in the MHRC encounter | 11

Enough of unpacking mobilization into the acts and processes that make it up. It's time to put it back together and look at careers as a whole. Some groups face handicaps that make skillful mobilizing acts necessary for success. Other groups don't need to do half as much to reach the same rebellious state. Here we explore how the various mobilizing acts interact with a group's starting point to produce its characteristic rebellion career.

Table 11–1 summarizes the major findings of the previous five chapters. Along the side, the groups are ranked by the outcome of their career—from fully mobilized quick starters to tractables whose rebellion never got off the ground. The columns include the most important variables affecting career. For each of our major processes, we have selected the most powerful predictor of ultimate success.

Multiple spokespersons in a group is our measure of adequate organizing. As we argued earlier, it is an important indicator of collective orientation. It marks a point at which the group is beginning to take such an orientation for granted. Each recurrence, and especially each fresh usage by a new person, embeds the orientation more deeply. If this organizing activity has occurred frequently before act 3, it has by then become only natural to treat the affidavit in a collective fashion.

Early context setting is our measure of adequate framing activity. It links a collective orientation with future action and provides a reason for resistance. By making the injustice frame a part of public discourse in the group, it promotes its shared adoption.

Early contract voiding is our measure of adequate breaking out from the bonds of authority. *Early* means by the end of act 1, before the first break scene occurs. If a group is still tacitly accepting an obligation at this point in the scenario, the difficulty of adequate framing and organizing activity is compounded. The continued tug of obligation distracts participants and inhibits the other necessary acts.

Early in this research, we sensed that a group's response to the first dilemma of compliance was critical for the rest of its career. The best group response at this point is rim talk. Rim talk is part of the process of breaking out, but it is difficult to sustain such an exchange without engaging in some reframing acts as well. Furthermore, rim talk frequently provides an occasion for organizing acts such as protest humor or speaking for the group. In short, it is a response that can set all of the critical processes in motion.

Table 11–1 also contains the bad news for rebellion careers. It includes the important prior conditions of unconducive climate and a know-how deficit. It also includes an important measure of a failure to develop a collective orientation—late, unresolved disagreements over compliance strategy in the final scenes before the act 3 showdown.

The story of this chapter, then, is summarized by Table 11–1. Not surprisingly, the successful groups in the upper left are dense with pluses; the minuses are mostly in the lower right among the least successful groups. But there are a number of more subtle patterns that cannot be so easily seen.

DOING EVERYTHING NECESSARY

Even a group with severe handicaps can succeed if it performs the proper mobilizing acts. There are only four groups that have pluses in every positive category, and they were uniformly successful. Perhaps the most striking case of all was the one with the most unconducive climate in the entire set of 33. In most groups, virtually no one believed that oil companies usually serve the public interest, but in this group, half the participants thought so. Similarly, the group showed attitude divisions on other relevant items such as the right of employers to be concerned about an employee's off-the-job behavior and the right of authorities to investigate the private lives of citizens.

Yet this group, in spite of its lack of prior consensus on the issues underlying the case of Mr. C., unanimously refused to sign the affidavit and made plans for future action as well. They did everything right. They engaged the coordinator in immediate rim talk, developed multiple spokespersons, voided the contract early enough, and performed the appropriate context setting. Consequently, the late, unresolved disagreements that one might have expected never came about. They reached the final act well prepared for a successful rebellion in spite of their initial handicap.

TABLE 11–1 Major variables affecting rebellion career

Type	Multiple spokespersons	Early context setting	Early contract voiding	Immediate rim talk	Late unresolved disagreements	Unconducive climate	Know-how deficit
Quick starter*	+	+	+	+			
Quick starter*	+	+	+	+			
Quick starter*		+	+	+			
Quick starter	+	+	+	+			
Quick starter		+	+	+			
Quick starter			+	+			
Quick starter			+	+			
Late bloomer*	+	+	+	+	−		
Late bloomer*	+		+				
Late bloomer†	+			+		−	
Late bloomer†	+	+		+			
Late bloomer†	+	+		+			
Late bloomer†		+	+	+			
Late bloomer	+			+			
Late bloomer	+		+				
Late bloomer			+				−

	1	2	3	4	5	6	7
Factional success†		−	−				
Factional success†		−	−	+		+	
Factional success†			−	+		+	
Factional success		−	−	+	+		
Factional success		−		+	+	+	
Factional success		−	−	+	+	+	
Factional success			−				
Factional success	−	−					
Factional success	−	−					
Fizzler	−	−	+	+	+	+	
Fizzler	−	−	+	+	+		
Fizzler	−		+				
Fizzler	−	−	+		+		
Tractable	−	−					
Tractable	−	−					
Tractable	−	−					
Tractable	−	−					

Note: + means activity occurred; − means problem was present.
* Group mobilized and took direct action.
† Group mobilized.

Most groups, however, failed on at least one of the three major processes. More than 40 percent of them went on to a successful career anyway, indicating that, while these mobilizing acts may be sufficient, they are not always necessary. These groups were successful because they had the good fortune not to face the special problems created by an unconducive climate. As Figure 11-1 indicates, a group has a 60 percent chance of success even with insufficient organizing, framing or divesting—*if it starts with the proper climate*. But it has little chance of success if it begins with the handicap of a less favorable climate and then neglects the appropriate mobilizing acts.

FIGURE 11-1   Climate by career for groups with
insufficient organizing, framing, or divesting

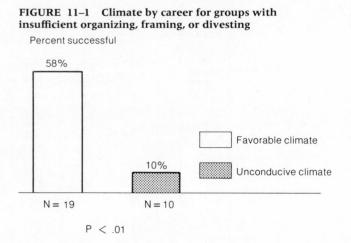

In some of these successful groups, the participants did not really develop a strong collective orientation, but were led to success by one or more exemplars. Lacking solidarity or a shared interpretation, they were highly vulnerable to the outbreak of disagement over how to respond. But given the like-mindedness of participants on the issues, they were capable of developing a shared definition of the situation and a unanimous response that would have been insufficient under less favorable initial conditions.

INSUFFICIENT KNOW-HOW AND ITS CONSEQUENCES

Even groups with a favorable climate have a need for know-how, and the need becomes more acute as the climate becomes less conducive. Note in Figure 11-2 the relative importance of know-how compared to climate in predicting immediate rim talk. The coordinator's request that some group members give opinions they didn't believe came as a surprise. The coordinator, who acted as if he took compliance for granted, was not easily engaged in a negotiation. Indeed, if a response was delayed only slightly, he accomplished his exit and the opportunity was lost.

FIGURE 11–2   Unfavorable conditions and rim talk

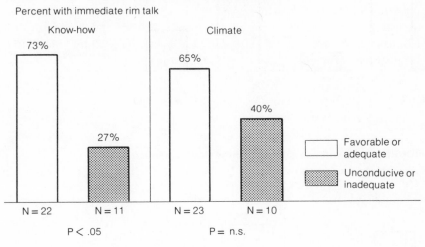

Percent with immediate rim talk

Know-how
73%

Climate
65%

40%

27%

Favorable or adequate

Unconducive or inadequate

N = 22   N = 11   N = 23   N = 10

P < .05   P = n.s.

In spite of these difficulties, almost three-fourths of the groups with adequate know-how were able to engage him in immediate rim talk. Only about one-fourth of the groups with a deficit in know-how passed this early test. In contrast, there was a much weaker relationship between climate and early rim talk. Prior attitudes toward oil companies and the like were not as relevant for this first step in breaking the bonds of authority.

Lack of know-how also led to failure in sufficient organizing activity. As Figure 11–3 shows, only one group with a deficit in know-how developed multiple spokespersons, but this state of collective orientation was reached in almost half of the others.

Lack of know-how may also hinder reframing. As Figure 11–4 shows, groups with a deficit tended to omit early context setting, but climate was a better predictor of this reframing act. Of the 17 groups that had neither deficit, 59 percent had early context setting; only 1 of the 5 groups with a double deficit achieved this benchmark of framing activity. Finally, neither know-how nor climate was very strongly related to early contract voiding. As Figure 11–5 shows, when either unfavorable condition was present, it seemed to slow the process of breaking out, but the results fall short of statistical significance.

FIGURE 11–3 Unfavorable conditions and organizing

Percent with multiple spokespersons

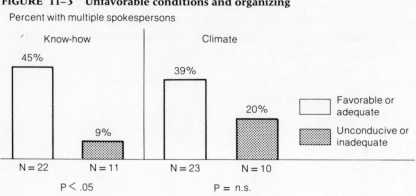

P < .05   P = n.s.

FIGURE 11–4 Unfavorable conditions and framing

Percent with early context setting

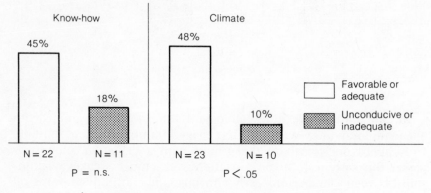

P = n.s.   P < .05

FIGURE 11–5 Unfavorable conditions and breaking out

Percent with early contract voiding

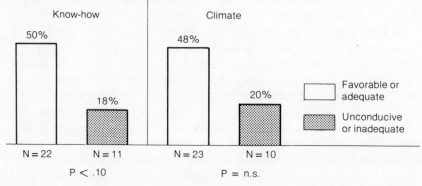

P < .10   P = n.s.

Our argument, then, is that a lack of know-how hinders a group in organizing and, to some degree, in reframing and breaking out as well. By their failure, these groups were extremely vulnerable to disagreements that are likely to arise among any group of relatively heterogeneous strangers. One might think that an unconducive climate would be a better predictor of late, unresolved disagreements. After all, we measured this variable by the presence of a subgroup that did not share general community standards about the relevant issues. Since there was no initial consensus, a late, unresolved disagreement might be expected.

In fact, it was a deficit in know-how that turned out to be the better predictor, as Figure 11–6 shows. It should come as no surprise that late, unresolved disagreements occurred in only 30 percent of the groups that began with the right climate. But they occurred in less than one-fourth of the groups with enough know-how. It was not consensus about oil companies that was important, because disagreements about how to handle the dilemmas would still be present to some degree. If groups lack people who can manage conflict and build solidarity, small conflicts may be enough to scramble the group's response when they face the critical dilemmas of compliance.

FIGURE 11–6 Unfavorable conditions and late, unresolved disagreements

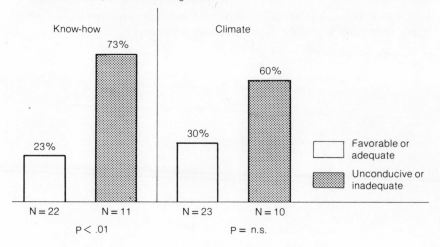

Percent with late, unresolved disagreements

SUMMARY

This completes our tale of the MHRC encounter. Some groups began with a sufficient number of members with the relevant know-how for this encounter, enabling most of them to produce the various mobilizing acts that led to a successful career.

More specifically, lacking a deficit they were likely to engage the coordinator in rim talk shortly after the first dilemma of compliance. This enabled the group to begin developing a collective orientation, build solidarity, and move toward a shared injustice frame. When exemplars arose, these groups were more likely to respond collectively and to avoid splits in rebellion strategy. Hence they were ready for a successful collective rebellion when the crucial test arose. They were loose from the bonds of authority, were aware that they shared the injustice frame, and had already established some tradition of responding collectively. They were prepared to pressure reluctant rebels to go along with the group.

If groups with sufficient know-how also start with a conducive climate, they may not need too much skill to succeed. With a certain amount of luck, a rebellious exemplar may find everyone willing to go along, especially if contract voiding occurs early and the group is largely free of the bonds of authority by the final act. There may still be some confusion, incomplete adoption of the injustice frame, and relatively weak solidarity, but no one in the group is inclined to challenge the exemplars.

Woe be it to the group that lacks know-how and a conducive climate. Lack of know-how means the critical mobilizing acts are unlikely to occur, and the less conducive climate means they are sorely needed. With some of the acts, the group may become a fizzler or even a factional success, but when all of the critical acts are absent, they are likely to remain tractable throughout their careers.

The theory and practice of rebellion | 12

A THEORY OF MICROMOBILIZATION

We have focused much more on *how* people rebel than on *why*. Indeed, we have taken the why for granted. Abuse of authority is the primary theme of the twentieth century, reaching full fruition in Nazi Germany; the Holocaust is its ultimate symbol. Given the myriad abuses of authority that we have all witnessed in our lifetimes, perhaps the more appropriate question is: Why do people not rebel?

The answer is that it is easier said than done. It requires active enterprise, frequently fraught with great risk, to rebel. The enterprise can falter at many points and for many reasons. In attempting to explain *how* groups forge a successful rebellion career, we are implicitly addressing the question of *why* people don't rebel. They falter on one of the many obstacles that can stifle or abort rebellious collective action.

Our explanation has two parts to it. On the one hand, every encounter has a certain context and assets that the participants have brought to it. These are a fixed starting point in any given encounter, but they are of major importance in understanding the problems and opportunities that potential challengers face under different circumstances.

The second part of our explanation is more dynamic. If we analyze the enterprise directly, focusing on a set of identifiable mobilizing acts, we see that each of these acts increases the overall capacity of the group for rebellious collective action in the encounter. We can unpack the overall process of mobilization into three simultaneous subprocesses, to show how the specific mobilizing acts further one or another

147

of these. Progress in each realm facilitates progress in the others, allowing them to interact in fostering a successful rebellion career. Under different circumstances, one or another of these processes may be especially problematic, but progress in each of them is necessary. Together, they are sufficient for a successful rebellion career—in the absence of active countermeasures by authorities. This is the logic of our explanation.

As for its content, we review the argument of the past several chapters, beginning with historical context. Encounters occur in a particular climate, sometimes conducive to rebellion and sometimes not. It is most conducive when there is both a recent history of rebellious action by other similar groups, plus sympathetic political authorities who support some of the collective goals and aspirations of the challengers.

Unconducive general climates may be neutralized or offset by particular local climates, as the Berkeley encounter illustrates. Berkeley is an example of what Moore calls "social and cultural space [that] provides a more or less protected enclave within which dissatisfied or oppressed groups have some room to develop distinctive social arrangements, cultural traditions, and explanations of the world around them" (1978: 482). Potential challengers, then, are not simply at the mercy of historical context but can, to some degree, create the climate that prevails in an encounter with unjust authority.

The concept of climate enables us to incorporate historical context, while cleavage pattern is our way of incorporating social context. We need to understand the extent to which underlying social cleavages in the society are being activated and made salient in the encounter. We suggest four different cleavage patterns, each with different implications for a successful rebellion career. In a *corresponding pattern*, no salient social cleavage partitions the authorities from the other participants. In effect, cleavage structure may be safely ignored in such encounters.

In a *reinforcing pattern*, relations of dominance and subordination present in the social context are reproduced in the encounter. This is especially complex because it has two competing effects on mobilization. On the one hand, a reinforcing pattern helps in the process of loyalty building because there is a salient "we" and "they." On the other hand, it retards the process of breaking out because the exercise of authority runs with the grain of custom.

In a *counteracting pattern*, the normal relationship of dominance and subordination is reversed in the encounter. It is a rare circumstance, but especially conducive for a successful career when it occurs. It is relatively easy to break out when authorities are of lower status than potential challengers. At the same time, positive effects on building loyalty are preserved, making it easier for potential challengers to work together.

The *dividing pattern* is the most difficult and intractable context for a successful rebellion career. Here, the salient cleavage divides people into a set that includes the authority and some potential challengers, and another set that includes the rest of the potential challengers. This greatly enhances the possibility of a split developing among potential challengers, in which a loyalist faction emerges in support of compliance. Potential challengers are highly vulnerable to efforts by authorities that stimulate internal division, paralyzing the ability of the group to act collectively. Furthermore, there is no easy basis for building collective identification. To achieve this, challengers must rely on more immediate, situational bonds among participants.

Both potential challengers and authorities bring certain assets to the encounter. For the authorities, these assets are the resources and know-how necessary to carry out social control routines. They bring to the encounter both a repertoire of routines and a certain level of skill in executing them. Similarly, potential challengers bring to an encounter assets for the enterprise of rebellion. It is not the relative amount of assets that each side has that is important, but the sufficiency of each side's assets for the task at hand. It is useful to think of a threshold of necessary assets of different types. An insufficiency at a given point will operate as a constraint on the possible courses of action that challengers or authorities may pursue. A deficit of know-how, for example, may mean that a group of potential challengers will lack necessary leadership in mobilizing a group for rebellious collective action.

Context and assets exist at the beginning of an encounter, but they do not determine its course. Much of what happens is in the hands of the participants, and they can affect its outcome by what they do in the course of the interaction. Our argument focuses on what potential challengers can do in furthering three processes that underlie mobilization: working together, breaking out of the bonds of authority, and adopting an injustice frame. Each process is advanced by different types of mobilizing acts: organizing, divesting, and reframing acts, respectively.

An *organizing act* is one that increases the capacity of the potential challengers to act as a unit. More specifically, these acts serve to build solidarity and loyalty to a challenging organization, create some procedure or apparatus for managing logistical problems, or manage internal conflicts so that they don't disrupt collective action.

A *divesting act* is one that weakens the bonds of authority. More specifically, these acts void obligations to authority, handle fears about making a scene, or personalize responsibility. Potential challengers are free of the bonds of authority when they no longer feel any obligations to comply, they are no longer concerned about disrupting the smooth flow of interaction, and they do not regard the authority system which lays its claim on them as beyond human agency. Considerations of self-interest may still be important, but they are psychologically free for participation in rebellious collective action.

A *reframing act* furthers the collective adoption of the injustice frame at the expense of the legitimating frame. It is accomplished through public acts that call attention to something wrong in what the authorities are doing (attention calling) and that link what is happening with an explicit injustice frame (context setting).

This, then, is our theory of micromobilization in encounters with unjust authority. The applicability of this theory to a range of cases was illustrated by an extended analysis of a few historical examples. We have tried to evaluate the theory more rigorously, by examining a series of hypotheses derived from it, to make sense of the variation in rebellion career among groups in the MHRC encounter. At this point, it is worth asking how well the theory fared in such a test.

EVALUATING THE THEORY

The 33 iterations of an encounter with the Manufacturers' Human Relations Consultants have given us an extraordinarily rich body of data. Flawed though our efforts may have been in achieving complete standardization, there is no set of naturally occurring encounters that even remotely approaches the degree of comparability of these cases. At the same time, the MHRC encounter retained most of the verisimilitude of naturally occurring encounters with unjust authority. It is hard to imagine any natural encounters in which one might have such fine-grained, systematic, and reliable observations on exactly what occurred, let alone 33 different instances with identical measurements of relevant variables.

The MHRC encounters do not enable us to shed light on every aspect of our theory. We have arguments concerning the relative difficulty of different cleavage structures, but the MHRC encounters were all corresponding patterns and can provide no enlightenment on these hypotheses. Furthermore, our theory is ex post facto, derived from a combination of our prior hunches and our impressions of what happened in the MHRC encounter. Our more systematic data analyses allowed us to check our impressions, and to discover that some of them were incorrect, but we make no claim that our theory was derived independently of the encounters it is being asked to explain.

Nevertheless, the variations in rebellion careers found in the MHRC encounter are not easy to explain, and we may ask how helpful our theory of micromobilization has been in making sense of the observed differences. We were successful in creating a generally favorable climate for mobilization, but this was neutralized in some groups by the presence of a subgroup with pro-MHRC sympathies. Our evidence suggests that a favorable climate is likely to mean fewer problems for a successful rebellion career, especially in learning to work together and agreeing on a common course of action.

Our evidence on assets supports the usefulness of the threshold argument. Resources were largely irrelevant in the MHRC encounter, but some know-how was required. The least successful groups—tractables and fizzlers—were particularly likely to be undersupplied with people who had the experiences and training that often produce know-how. At the same time, there is no evidence at all that having a large number of people with high education and political experiences gave a group any special advantage. Our evidence supports the view that, with respect to assets, enough is enough.

Our theory points to certain processes as relevant and suggests a series of individual mobilizing acts that further each process. In effect, we hypothesized that the performance of these specified acts before the affidavit scene—and as early as possible—would be associated with collective resistance or preparation for future action after this point. Most of these hypotheses were supported, sometimes strikingly so.

Quick starters were especially fast in adopting an injustice frame and breaking out. They were very quick in attention calling and relatively early and more frequent in context setting and contract voiding. In contrast, they were not especially early or frequent in organizing acts, even lagging behind the late bloomers somewhat in this process. It is worth noting that three of the factional successes would have met our criteria as quick starters had they succeeded later in achieving collective resistance. Perhaps it is possible to act too quickly. In a favorable climate, early acts of resistance and confrontation with the coordinator propelled a rebellion career forward, but in a less favorable climate they were premature. They failed to draw all of the potential challengers into the rebellion and to forestall the emergence of a compliant minority faction, who signed the affidavit.

Late bloomers were slower to break out and adopt the injustice frame but they did so quite adequately in act 2. In a sense, the three processes were better synchronized in these groups. There had been more time for loyalty-building acts to occur and for the group to develop its capacity for working together. With this advance work, divesting acts were less likely to stimulate an internal conflict over handling the dilemmas of compliance.

Factional successes were almost as rapid and complete in breaking out as the late bloomers—in some cases, even faster. They were, however, considerably weaker in organizing and reframing than the successful groups, and more likely to have late, unresolved disagreements. Had these groups developed a stronger collective orientation, they might have been readier to discuss what was happening. Had they been able to reach collective adoption of the injustice frame, then they might more easily have resolved the strategy disagreements that arose later. But in the absence of the organizing and reframing acts that would have promoted these developments, they were especially vulnerable to a later split.

The fizzlers in our sample remain a fascinating set of groups. On some mobilizing acts, they were comparable to our successful groups, and only one of the four had an unfavorable climate. They tended to start well, usually with immediate rim talk, and they had pretty well broken out by the middle of act 2. But every one of them had a deficit in know-how, and most of them had multiple deficits. This lack of know-how meant that important organizing or reframing acts failed to occur. This left them highly vulnerable to late disagreements that arose in most of them. These groups appeared to lose their nerve and become frightened by their own early defiance. Some participants began to make amends to the coordinator and drew others toward what eventually became collective compliance instead of resistance.

Finally, the tractables were weak on all of the processes. They made a respectable showing on attention calling, but were very weak on context setting. They were late to begin rim talk, and their contract voiding occurred very late if at all. They were low on loyalty-building acts and failed to resolve the conflicts that arose. In the end, they failed to make much progress on any of the necessary processes for a successful rebellion career, and ended up giving the MHRC pretty much what it asked for.

In sum, groups with different careers did mobilize at different rates, as suggested by our theory. The theory focuses on differences that led groups to different careers, and it accounts in a coherent fashion for the overall pattern of results.

THE PRACTICE OF REBELLION

Sooner or later, many of us will confront a situation in which we are part of a group faced with one or more dilemmas of compliance. Our theory has practical implications for such encounters. It tells us what to do if we want to succeed in fomenting rebellious collective action. It suggests a how-to manual for rebellion.

One begins by assessing the special vulnerabilities and opportunities that stem from context. With respect to climate, ask how generally supportive it is for potential challengers. If the climate is favorable, you are fortunate and need not worry about it. If it is not favorable, this means that divesting and reframing will require extra attention. The legitimating frame may be expected to seem especially natural and taken-for-granted and the bonds of authority to be especially strong.

One must also assess cleavage structure, determining which pattern prevails. If it is a corresponding pattern, you don't need to worry about it. If it is a reinforcing pattern, you have both an opportunity and an obstacle. The opportunity comes in loyalty building; you can use the common social position to facilitate a sense of common fate. But it is an obstacle to breaking out, and this process will require extra care and attention. If the cleavage pattern is counteracting, you are fortunate again and need not worry about it; it will work for you. If it is a dividing pattern, you have a difficult task and should try to de-emphasize the cleavage as much as possible. If you are successful in this regard, you will have transformed the unfavorable dividing pattern into a more neutral, corresponding pattern.

Assets also require a careful assessment. For resources, it is a matter of determining whether or not what you need is present. In many cases, resource needs are minimal and can be ignored, but the absence of any that might be needed is a constraint. The form of action that you pursue needs to reflect this constraint. If you have read this book, you should now have the necessary repertoire; you can help the group to rebel, as well as polish your skills, by applying this knowledge.

The basic practice of rebellion is to make sure that the various mobilizing acts are performed. When an agent of authority acts in a manner that is questionable, make sure that someone calls attention to it. Even if others probably noticed it, calling attention not only makes sure of this, but, more importantly, it makes everyone aware that it is common knowledge.

Perhaps the problematic behavior will be remedied, in which case no injustice frame is appropriate. Then there is no particular need for mobilizing rebellious collective action. Our advice is intended for a situation in which the agent continues to operate in a way that is likely to produce an injustice. The injustice frame makes sense of the agent's behavior by showing that it is consistent with some objective that the authority system is actively seeking.

A full-fledged injustice frame may not be immediately clear. You may not understand the full context of the authority's behavior without discussion and probing. Consider the development of an injustice frame to be a collective problem, not merely your personal one, and enlist the help of other potential challengers in analyzing the context. Press the agents of authority for the information that would help to make the context clearer. Your objective is to facilitate the *shared* definition of the situation as one in which the unimpeded operation of the authority system will result in an injustice.

It may be difficult in many encounters to find the time and space for a detailed discussion and analysis, but we don't suggest that rebellion is easy. One is apt to be facing active efforts at social control, not the passivity of the MHRC coordinator. Divesting acts deal with the inevitable confrontation between a group attempting to mobilize, and authorities attempting to gain their compliance.

Authorities frequently have sanctions available to back up their efforts at gaining voluntary compliance. Premature acts of protest may isolate challengers and make them vulnerable to such sanctions. Overt acts of protest are appropriate when the process of breaking out is close to completion, but they can easily backfire if the bonds of authority are still intact.

The first step in breaking out is rim talk, in which the terms and conditions of compliance are actively negotiated, not merely accepted as the natural prerogative of authority. This step weakens several different bonds simultaneously. First, it preserves the face of the particular agent of authority, allowing divesting to proceed without disrupting the smooth flow of interaction any more than necessary. Second, it either forces into the open or undercuts reification. If the rules are a subject of negotiation and can be altered, then they are not independent of human agency. While such rim talk involves making a contract explicit and negotiating its terms, it does not directly void obligation. But it is likely to provide the basis for later voiding it, by providing a basis for the claim that authorities are operating in violation of its terms. Finally, rim talk is less likely than more overt acts of protest to provide a justification for sanctions—although some authorities might treat it as a sufficient provocation in itself. It does not eliminate risk, but it reduces it.

If authorities refuse to negotiate or if the negotiations break down, it is easier to move then to more advanced acts of protest that void the obligation of potential challengers to comply. An individual act of resistance indicates that a particular person does not feel obliged to comply, but making the claim explicit and public declares it void for other potential challengers as well. If the reframing process has properly advanced, an injustice frame may itself serve as the justification for voiding any obligation to comply.

If potential challengers have some prior history of working together, this existing organizational structure may be useful in enabling them to find a unified course of action. In many encounters, however, the potential challengers have little prior experience in working together, and this process will require active effort. Part of your job as an organizer in this situation would be to foster a sense of collective identity. If there is an explicit challenging organization involved, then act in the name of it so that potential challengers will recognize it as a carrier of their interests and values.

Be alert to the logistics of collective action. Procedural suggestions at various points will enable challengers to carry out the collective action routines that they consider. Finally, give explicit attention to the handling of disagreements in a way that allows a group to proceed. If one can't find a common course of action on which participants can agree, there are other procedures besides consensus. A straw vote or a show of hands may convince a minority faction to support a course of action that has clear majority support. Voting is a widely recognized and legitimated mechanism for resolving conflicts, and can serve even in ad hoc groups that have no life beyond a single encounter.

CONCLUSION

There are not likely to be break scenes in unfabricated encounters with unjust authority. Rather than a series of dilemmas of compliance, spread over time, one may unexpectedly confront a single one without lead time to do mobilizing work. And real-life authorities are usually much more active than the MHRC was in its use of social control measures. It is no surprise, then, that rebellious collective action is so much rarer than the injustices at which it is occasionally directed.

Nevertheless, it takes enterprise and courage to rebel—even against the Manufacturers' Human Relations Consultants. One may not need iron in the soul, but, at least, some heavy-duty aluminum foil there. Much of what has been written on obedience to authority emphasizes the willingness of people to comply, even when such compliance involves serious injury to others. But this wasn't true in the MHRC encounters.

Perhaps the most hopeful message in our account is the frequency with which ordinary people, with no prior experience of working together, were able to join together in actively resisting an unjust authority. Only a handful of groups gave the MHRC what it wanted throughout the encounter. In more than three quarters of them, most people ended up overtly resisting the unjust authority.

Sometimes they did so with a rhetoric that invoked past images of discredited complicity. Watergate and Eichmann were raised as examples of wrongful compliance, and the Milgram fabrication was referred to in four different groups. They drew a lesson from these exemplars: people should resist unjust authority. Although earlier studies have suggested that people are overly compliant, our message is a complementary one: people sometimes resist unjust authority when they should, and we can all learn from their efforts in doing so.

Appendix | A
Questionnaires

I. **Initial questionnaire**

As part of a larger study of community attitudes, we are asking for your cooperation in completing this questionnaire. You will be asked to express your opinions on a number of issues. After completing the questionnaire, you and the other participants will have an opportunity to discuss some of the issues more fully. Thank you for your cooperation.

Below are pairs of statements on a variety of issues. Check the one that comes closer to how you feel about the issue. On some issues you may strongly agree with one of the statements; but on other issues neither statement may come very close to your feelings. Even if you don't fully agree with either, *please check one and only one statement* from each pair. Then indicate how strongly you agree with the statement that you checked.

 1. _____The policies of the large oil companies usually harm the public interest.
_____The policies of the large oil companies usually serve the public interest.
How strongly do you agree with the statement you have checked?
_____Strongly agree. _____Moderately agree. _____Barely agree.

 2. _____Employees are treated fairly by most businesses.
_____Most businesses take advantage of their employees.
How strongly do you agree with the statement you have checked?
_____Strongly agree. _____Moderately agree. _____Barely agree.

3.   _____What an employee does on his own time should *not* concern his employer.

     _____Employers have a right to be concerned if an employee's off-the-job behavior offends the community.

     How strongly do you agree with the statement you have checked?

     _____Strongly agree. _____Moderately agree. _____Barely agree.

4.   _____Authorities should have the right to investigate the private lives of citizens.

     _____The right of authorities to investigate the private lives of citizens must be severely limited.

     How strongly do you agree with the statement you have checked?

     _____Strongly agree. _____Moderately agree. _____Barely agree.

5.   _____There is too much respect for authority in America nowadays.

     _____There is not enough respect for authority in America nowadays.

     How strongly do you agree with the statement you have checked?

     _____Strongly agree. _____Moderately agree. _____Barely agree.

6.   _____I often have difficulty knowing what is right and what is wrong.

     _____I seldom have difficulty knowing what is right and what is wrong.

     How strongly do you agree with the statement you have checked?

     _____Strongly agree. _____Moderately agree. _____Barely agree.

7.   _____I wouldn't mind if I had to associate with an individual who is having a sexual affair.

     _____I would feel uncomfortable if I had to associate with an individual who is having a sexual affair.

     How strongly do you agree with the statement you have checked?

     _____Strongly agree. _____Moderately agree. _____Barely agree.

8.   Generally speaking, how much do you think we can trust the *courts* to do what is right?

     _____Just about always. _____Most of the time. _____Some of the time. _____Almost never.

9.   Generally speaking, how much do think we can trust the *government in Washington* to do what is right?

     _____Just about always. _____Most of the time. _____Some of the time. _____Almost never.

10. How often do you talk about public affairs and political issues to other people?

     _____Nearly every day. _____Once or twice a week. _____Rarely. _____Never.

11. On most political issues, would you say you are on the liberal side, on the conservative side, or middle-of-the-road?

     _____Liberal. _____Conservative. _____Middle-of-the-road.

12. Let's say that you are working for a company that insists you and your co-workers do something which is not part of your job, and which you do not want to do.
    What would you do about it?
    Let's say that you did that. How likely is it that your action would solve the problem?
    _____Very likely. _____A fair possibility. _____Very unlikely.

13. Let's say that there's a problem in your community that bothers you a lot. You've approached the local authorities about the problem, but they've done nothing. Which of the following would you be most likely to do next?
    _____Nothing.
    _____Get together with other people who are also upset, and try to do something about the problem.
    _____Try to do something on an individual basis.
    _____Move out of the community.

14. Let's say the problem is that more and more unmarried couples are living together in your community. You feel that this way of living is immoral, and it bothers you a lot. What would you be most likely to do about it?
    _____Nothing.
    _____Get together with other people who also are upset, and try to do something about the problem.
    _____Try to do something about the problem on an individual basis.
    _____Move out of the community.

Please check the highest level of education you have had:
_____Less than 9th grade   _____Some college
_____Some high school   _____Graduated college
_____Graduated high school   _____Some graduate school

Listed below are several kinds of clubs and organizations that some people belong to. Have you belonged to any clubs or organizations at any time during the past five years?
_____Yes, _____No

If you have, please write the names of the specific clubs and organizations next to the appropriate category below. For example, if you are a member of the Teamsters Union, you may write "Teamsters" in the blank next to labor union.
Neighborhood club or association _____
Church or church connected group _____
Fraternal organization or lodge _____
Business, professional, or civic association _____
Political organization or club _____
Labor union _____
Sports club or group _____

PTA _____
Veterans Organization _____
Other (please specify) _____
After you have written in the names of any specific clubs and
organizations you have belonged to, please circle the names of
those in which you have been very active.

II. **Posthoax questionnaire**

Please answer the following questions as completely as possible.

1. What bothered you the most about the Manufacturers' Human
    Relations Consultants (MHRC)? Why was that? Was there any-
    thing else that particularly bothered you?

2. How did you feel about the Manufacturers' Human Relations Con-
    sultants (MHRC) coordinator? Did you like or dislike him? Why
    was that?

3. What did you think the Manufacturers' Human Relations Consul-
    tants (MHRC) wanted from this group? Why do you think they
    were doing this research?

4. Did you ever suspect that the Manufacturers' Human Relations
    Consultants (MHRC) was not what it claimed to be? If you did
    suspect this, what made you suspicious and when was this?

5. What did you think was really happening?

6. When you were leaving what were you planning to do?

7. Here is a list of several activities you may have done in the past.
    Please check *all* the activities you have ever participated in and also
    indicate whether you were particularly active.

	Were you particularly active?
Check here if you ever:	Write yes or no.
A._____participated in a protest de-monstration?	_____
B._____attended political meetings or rallies?	_____
C._____participated in a wildcat strike?	_____
D._____participated in a strike author-ized by a union?	_____
E._____worked for a political candidate?	
F._____wrote letters to public officials or newspapers giving your political opinion?	_____

G._____challenged the order of a   _____
policeman, teacher, or em-
ployer?

H._____any other activity where you   _____
challenged someone's authority
over you?
Briefly describe what you did.   _____

Use the following scale to answer questions 8–13

1	2	3	4	5	6	7

Very   Not at
much   all

[Participants received a grid with the names of each participant in the columns.]

8. How opposed was each person to the Manufacturers' Human Relation Consultants (MHRC) and its procedures?

9. How useful were each person's ideas for dealing with the situation?

10. How concerned was each person with the feelings of the other group members?

11. How much were each person's thoughts and feelings *like your own?*

12. How much did you like each of the other persons?

13. How much did each person influence how you dealt with the situation?

14. Did you know this person before you came here today? Indicate yes or no and briefly describe how you know them.

Answer questions 15–20 for each of the actions listed below: [Participants were provided with a matrix with questions in the columns and actions in the rows.]

15. Did it ever occur to you to do this?

16. Do you think this would have been a *good* idea?

17. Do you think this would have been wrong?

18. Do you think this would have gotten you into too much trouble?

19. Do you think this would have taken too much effort?

20. How many people would have had to go along with you before you'd have done this?

Actions:

a. Taking the participation forms.

b. Confronting or threatening the coordinator.

c. Going to some outside authority to have them stop the research.

d. Going along with the MHRC procedures and finishing the research.

     e.   Going to some outside organization to investigate the MHRC.

     f.   Trying harder to get the coordinator to change the procedures or make compromises.

     g.   Taking the videotapes or trying to erase them.

     h.   Refusing to sign the final release form (affidavit).

21.   Do you have any misgivings about having participated in this experiment? Please explain.

III. **Six-month follow-up questionnaire**

---

1.   Looking back on the experience of having participated, do you have any misgivings about having done so?
(Check one)   _____Yes   _____No

2.   Do you feel that you learned anything from participating?
(Check one)   _____Yes   _____No

3.   Do you feel that you were exploited?
(Check one)   _____Yes   _____No
If yes, in what way do you feel that you were exploited?

4.   If you can still recall, how much stress did you experience during your participation?
(Check one)
_____Can't recall.
_____No more stress than one might expect to encounter in an average day.
_____More stress than one is likely to encounter in an average day.
_____More stress than one is likely to encounter in an average month.
_____The most stressful experience I have encountered in the last year.

5.   In presenting this research to colleagues and students, we may wish to show them a videotape of a discussion. Please indicate how you feel about our using the videotape in which you appear for such purposes.
(Check one)
_____I prefer that you don't use the videotape in which I appear.
_____I don't mind if you use the videotape in which I appear.
_____I am pleased to have you use the videotape in which I appear.
(Please use reverse side for additonal comments you would like to make.)

Appendix | B
Coding procedures and reliability

For reasons described in chapter 3, we greatly shortened the data collection phase of this research. This left us with additional time and resources which we chose to invest in a very elaborate coding operation lasting almost 18 months. Our basic coding device consisted of a standardized, play-by-play description of the videotaped interaction. Not all utterances were relevant for our codes, but for those that were we coded who said what to whom with up to two modifiers. The modifiers varied depending on the nature of the "what." For example, the utterance might consist of a refusal to give false opinions, with a modifier for tone (deferent, neutral, agitated, defiant, frivolous) and for the nature of the specific grievance (negative consequences for Mr. C., for example). Hence any given utterance received a field of as many as five different codes.

Not all of our coding was done in a single wave, but the major part of it—focusing on compliance-relevant acts—followed the format described above. For this main wave, the tapes were coded twice by independent coders, and a third person reconciled any disagreements, reviewing the tape if necessary. Hence we acquired voluminous data on coding reliability.

There were a number of different criteria of reliability. If one asks how often both coders included the utterance and coded it in exactly the same fashion throughout the entire field, the answer is about 70 percent of the time. However, this figure greatly underrates the reliability of the measures reported in this study, because many disagreements were inconsequential. One coder, for example, might have coded a remark as addressed to the whole group, while the other coded it as addressed to a single individual—a disagreement that played no role in our subsequent analysis.

The tone code described above proved insufficiently reliable. A better measure of reliability concerned agreement in how to code the *nature* of the utterance—that is, the what portion of the total field for that utterance. Here, the overall reliability averaged around 90 percent. It is somewhat higher than this for codes actually used in the analysis since certain distinctions in the original code proved difficult to make reliably, and some closely adjacent categories were later combined in our analysis. In sum, our coders missed little that was relevant for our analysis of rebellion career and were able to agree quite reliably on the coding of what occurred.

References

Alinsky, Saul (1972) *Rules for Radicals.* New York: Random House, Vintage Books.

Aminzade, Ronald (1977) "Breaking the Chains of Dependency: From Patronage to Class Politics." *Journal of Urban History* 3: 485–506.

Aveni, A. (1977) "The Not-So-Lonely Crowd: Friendship Groups in Collective Behavior." *Sociometry* 40 (March): 96–99.

Bok, Sisella (1978) *Lying.* New York: Pantheon Books.

Coleman, James S. (1974) *Power and the Structure of Society.* New York: W. W. Norton.

Coleman, James S. (1980) "Authority Systems." *Public Opinion Quarterly* 44 (Summer): 143–62.

Collins, Randall (1981) "On the Microfoundations of Macrosociology." *American Journal of Sociology* 86 (March): 984–1013.

Dahl, Robert A. (1957) "The Concept of Power." *Behavioral Science* 2 (July): 201–18.

Fine, Sidney (1969) *Sit-Down.* Ann Arbor: University of Michigan Press.

Gamson, William A. (1968) *Power and Discontent.* Homewood, Ill.: Dorsey Press.

Gamson, William A. (1975) *The Strategy of Social Protest.* Homewood, Ill.: Dorsey Press.

Gerlach, Luther P., and Hine, Virginia H. (1970) *People, Power, Change: Movements of Social Transformation.* Indianapolis: Bobbs-Merrill.

Gitlin, Todd (1977) "Spotlights and Shadows: Television and the Culture of Politics." *College English* (April).

Gitlin, Todd (1980) *The Whole World is Watching.* Berkeley: University of California Press.

Goffman, Erving (1959) *The Presentation of Self in Everyday Life.* New York: Doubleday Anchor Books.

Goffman, Erving (1961) *Encounters,* Indianapolis: Bobbs-Merrill.

Goffman, Erving (1974) *Frame Analysis.* Cambridge, Mass.: Harvard University Press.

Gray, Bradford H. (1975) *Human Subjects in Medical Experimentation.* New York: John Wiley & Sons.

Heirich, Max (1971) *The Spiral of Conflict; Berkeley, 1964.* New York: Columbia University Press.

Hirschman, Albert O. (1970) *Exit, Voice, and Loyalty.* Cambridge, Mass.: Harvard University Press.

Holmes, David S. (1976) "Debriefing after Psychological Experiments." *American Psychologist* 31 (December): 858–75.

Jenkins, J. Craig (1981) "Sociopolitical Movements." In *Handbook of Political Science,* edited by Samuel Long. Plenum Press.

Kelman, Herbert (1968) *A Time to Speak.* San Francisco: Jossey Bass.

Kraus, Henry (1947) *The Many and the Few.* Los Angeles: Plantin.

Malcolm X (with the assistance of Alex Haley) (1965) *The Autobiography of Malcolm X.* New York: Grove Press.

McCarthy, John D., and Zald, Mayer N. (1977) "Resource Mobilization in Social Movements: A Partial Theory." *American Journal of Sociology* 82 (May): 1212–34.

Milgram, Stanley (1974) *Obedience to Authority.* New York: Harper & Row (Harper Colophon.)

Molotch, Harvey (1979) "Media and Movements." in *The Dynamics of Social Movements,* edited by Mayer N. Zald and John D. McCarthy. Cambridge, Mass.: Winthrop Publishers.

Moore, Barrington, Jr. (1978) *Injustice: The Social Bases of Obedience and Revolt.* White Plains, N.Y.: M. E. Sharpe.

Oberschall, Anthony (1973) *Social Conflict and Social Movements.* Englewood Cliffs, N.J.: Prentice-Hall.

Piven, Frances Fox, and Cloward, Richard A. (1977) *Poor People's Movements.* New York: Vintage Books (Random House).

Rogers, Mary (1974) "Instrumental and Infra-Resources: The Bases of Power." *American Journal of Sociology* 79 (No. 6): 1418–33.

Ross, Robert J. (1978) "Primary Groups in Social Movements: A Memoir and Interpretation." *Journal of Voluntary Action Research* 6 (September).

Roy, Alice Myers (1978) *Irony in Conversation.* Ph.D. dissertation, University of Michigan.

Sennett, Richard (1980) *Authority.* New York: Alfred A. Knopf.

Schmeidler, Emilie (1980) *Shaping Ideas and Action: CORE, SCLC, and SNCC in the Struggle for Equality, 1960–66.* Ph.D. dissertation, University of Michigan.

Shorter, Edward, and Tilly, Charles (1974) *Strikes in France, 1830–1968.* Cambridge: Cambridge University Press.

Snyder, David, and Kelly, William R. (1976) "Industrial Violence in Italy, 1878–1903." *American Journal of Sociology* 82 (July): 131–62.

Tilly, Charles (1973) "The Chaos of the Living City." In *Violence as Politics,* edited by Herbert Hirsch and David C. Perry. New York: Harper & Row.

Tilly, Charles (1978) *From Mobilization to Revolution,* Reading, Mass.: Addison-Wesley.

Tilly, Charles (1979) "Repertoires of Contention in America and Britain, 1750–1830." Chapter in *The Dynamics of Social Movements,* by Mayer N. Zald and John McCarthy. Cambridge, Mass.: Winthrop Publishers.

Turner, Ralph, and Killian, Lewis (1972) *Collective Behavior.* Englewood Cliffs, N.J.: Prentice-Hall.

Walzer, Michael (1970) *Obligations,* Cambridge, Mass.: Harvard University Press.

Warwick, Donald P. (1975) "Deceptive Research: Social Scientists Ought to Stop Lying." *Psychology Today* 8 (February): 38–40, 105–06.

Zajonc, Robert B. (1980) "Feeling and Thinking: Preferences Need No Inferences." *American Psychologist* 35 (February): 151–75.

Zald, Mayer N., and McCarthy, John D., eds. (1979) *The Dynamics of Social Movements.* Cambridge, Mass.: Winthrop Publishers.

Zimbardo, Philip G.; Bantes, W. Curtis; Haney, Craig; and Jaffe, David (1973) "A Pirandellian Prison." *New York Times Magazine* (April 8) 38–40.

Index

This book has been set VIP, in 10 and 9 point Meridien Light, leaded 2 points. Chapter numbers and titles are 30 and 16 point Meridien Medium, respectively. The size of the type page is 26 by 46 picas.